GW00778089

Why Tilbury?

David Batchelor

WHY TILBURY?

JONATHAN CAPE
THIRTY-TWO BEDFORD SQUARE LONDON

First published 1985
Copyright © 1985 by David Batchelor

Jonathan Cape Ltd, 32 Bedford Square, London WC1

British Library Cataloguing in Publication Data

Batchelor, David
Why Tilbury?
1. England – Nobility – History
I. Title
305.5'223'0942   HT653.G7

ISBN 0-224-02320-9

The author and publishers would like to thank the following for permission
to reproduce copyright material: Hutchinson Books Ltd for the sonnet on
p. 12 by Rosamond Batchelor from Denzil Batchelor's autobiography,
Babbled of Green Fields; the Hogarth Press for Rae Dalven's translation of
C.P. Cavafy's *Ithaka*; and the Soncino Press Ltd and Birkbeck Montagu's
for Dr J.H. Hertz's *Commentary on the Pentateuch and Haftorahs.*

Typeset by Columns of Reading
Printed in Great Britain by St Edmundsbury Press
Bury St Edmunds, Suffolk

To Tom and Anthea

Chapter One

SNIPE, the gamekeeper, crushed the lingering bird's head in his hand. His hands were rough and red like raw steaks.

'They'll be coming over you this drive, my lord.'

The guns stood in a shallow valley below a wood of larches, pines and beeches. They had been waiting for nearly twenty minutes. It was warm for October. Lord Lingfield in tweeds mopped at his face with a red spotted handkerchief. From the depths of the wood there came a low booming that signalled the approach of the slowly advancing beaters. Lord Lingfield thought of Zulu warriors drumming on their shields. He kicked at a clod with his heavy leather boot. There had been no rain for weeks. Now the beaters' cries could be heard and the crack of their sticks against the trees. The gun dogs were itchy and impatient. And then, almost unexpectedly, there was a crescendo of clattering and suddenly a great belt of birds thundered into the sky. Lord Lingfield jerked his gun upwards and the birds streamed over him, safe and sound.

'What the hell's Bliss Lingfield playing at? He's been shooting like a townee all morning.'

A gun down the line, possibly Boy Athlone, brought down a straggler with a seemingly impossible swinging backwards shot. The bird clawed its way through the air and hit the ground with a thud. Snipe grinned. He was a ruddy-faced man who had earned his nickname at an early age for his love of gamebirds.

'Not your day, my lord.'

'No excuse, but I've got this damn pain in my back.'

'Dare say that spared the birds one.'

Luncheon was in a stone-flagged farmhouse. The eight guns sat at a round table eating cold steak and kidney pie. Conversation, which was sporadic and staccato, favoured the events of the morning. The host, Lord Framlingham, made heavy weather of small talk with the oldest man in the room, an attaché from the Austrian Embassy, who alone among the guns was paying for his day's pleasure. The others, while conceding with bated breath that the fellow might be a gent, questioned his shooting manners which were clearly continental. Boy Athlone claimed that twice that morning he had had to take evasive action because of the European's low-swinging gun. Bliss started to laugh, then looked pained. His neighbour, a small, beaming man thirty-five years in the cavalry, smacked him on the shoulder.

'Joined the anti blood sports league, old boy?'

'Not actually.'

The neighbour snorted and flushed, then rammed more food into his mouth. Gravy dappled his chin.

'You must be in love again then. You know what they say, lucky in love ... '

Bliss's pallid complexion was accentuated by the glossy blackness of his hair. A drooping moustache, fleshy lips and heavy eyelids made him, except on the infrequent occasions when he laughed or smiled, look sullen. His ex-wife Moyra had been unkind, but not untruthful, when she had likened his eyes to haemophiliac oysters.

Two limber girls, slightly breathless from being so vivacious, entered from the kitchen to clear the table and to set upon it a dish of pears stewed in red wine, and a Stilton. The host with apparent reluctance interrupted his conversation with the Austrian attaché (it concerned the ECFAT sugar-beet quota controversy) to go in search of the port. Boy Athlone nudged Bliss.

'Back playing you up? Want to see somebody about that. Pinkie Hamilton had the same trouble. Went to a doctor. Never walked again. Tip from my broker – Glastonbury Oil. Place is stiff with it. Got to keep the preservationists out, somehow.'

Exhausted by this lengthy speech, Boy bolted a pear and beadily eyed the slowly circulating port.

Snipe, who had eaten his dinner of sandwiches and bottled beer with the beaters in a derelict barn, came in with a scrap of paper. He handed it to the host who once more regretfully tore himself away from the attaché's conversation. His guests turned to him with avidity, a pack of scenting, tail-wagging beagles.

'Not quite up to scratch. Four hares, three brace of French partridge, one English, two snipe, a couple of woodcock, fourteen brace of pheasant and one rabbit. We'll take the Millfield cover first this afternoon. Better luck, gentlemen.'

He looked down the table to Bliss and smiled.

The setting sun veiled by evening mist was the colour of a grapefruit when the shoot ended. All the participants, dead and alive, paraded in the yard of the great house. Snipe had lined up both the game and the beaters with an attention to orderliness that a Regimental Sergeant-Major would have commended. In the front, three rows of pheasant, then a row of partridge, a row of woodcock, and at the back, the row of beaters – deferential men waiting to be paid, many of them cap in hand. The gun dogs and the guns looked on, sniffling and shuffling, impatient for food and whisky respectively. Lord Framlingham walked down the line of beaters. He had a reward and a word for each.

'Good to see you back on your feet, Charlie.'

'Missus well, Albert? Mind you don't drink it all.'

'First time out, young fellow? Enjoy yourself?'

Bliss stood by the ranks of the dead. A cock pheasant, most of its dandy feathers blasted away, had attracted the frenzied interest of a bluebottle. It scurried among the bird's bloodied craters, seeking, perhaps, the perfect nursery in which to lay its young.

A buck hare, inelegantly thrown down on its back, abruptly reminded Bliss of a disgrace at school long ago. Five or six of them, large boys, almost men, had chased a small boy down a passage into the last room. He remembered that at the time he had partly enjoyed the spectacle, partly been shocked by it. Snipe thrust a brace of pheasant into his hands. Bliss thanked him and gave him a tenner. There had been the suggestion of a pagan blood sacrifice. He couldn't be certain now whether the officiating priest had been Walton or Russell. As for the victim he could recollect neither his name nor his face.

He looked about the yard: the beaters were drifting away, the guns were chatting to the host, Snipe with the help of a boy was collecting the game to hang in the larder. He was struck by the sense of his own separateness. It had happened before – it was a horrifying knowledge. He wondered if he was going mad. In London, he would walk, sometimes all day, to obliterate the consciousness that he was alive. Or to forget that he would one day die. Somehow, to staunch the awareness that he existed.

'Bliss, that was a fine stag you killed on Fhada last August. Better have someone take a look at your back, old boy.'

Chapter Two

BEL, Bliss's paternal aunt, was blind to wealth. 'I have always been materially impoverished and spiritually opulent.' Unlike most fervent Catholics, she was not a convert. From early adulthood, she had lived in a companionable way with a succession of rich, pious old ladies. Now that she had survived them all, she was quite content with her two damp, draughty rooms and no bath in a tenement block close by the Embankment. For company she relied upon the telephone and a capuchin monkey. 'As a Catholic, what other pet could I possibly have?' She was a woman of strong principles, but, though she would have denied it, her religious scruples were never able to usurp her loyalty to her family. 'Bliss darling, I never once had faith in your marriage, and you know how empty anything is that lacks faith.' A vegetarian, her body and breath exuded the scent of pastoral goodness.

Whenever her nephew Bliss was at home in London, she rang him at noon; not only because she enjoyed talking to him, but also because she knew that her regularity annoyed him. It was noon now.

'Bliss dear, a pleasant weekend, I hope?'

'Father used to say that only hairdressers had weekends, but actually it was rather awful.'

'If you must massacre the creation, what else can you expect?'

'I meant, I felt awful.'

'Karma, pure karma.'

In spite of Bel's poverty, her bed-sitting-room was hung with an enviable collection of paintings: two Blakes, three Calverts and several Shoreham-period Palmers. None of the family knew how she had acquired them.

11

'How's Francis?'

'Fine. He's sitting on the bookcase nibbling fruit and playing with his nuts.'

Francis was Bel's capuchin. He had been named after her favourite saint and had been so christened by a Californian nun, albeit deprived. Long ago her tenement block association had tried to evict Francis, but Bel had successfully argued that their prohibition specifically only covered cats, dogs, mice, rabbits and inebriates. Prohibition or no prohibition, she had reminded them, the building abounded in cockroaches and silverfish. Few of the residents ever spoke to her, but she claimed it made no difference to her as they were all old or cantankerous or both.

'I suppose you'd like me to come and see you some time?'

'Bliss, how unlike you to be so graciously available. What do you want – money? You know I never have that.'

'I hate life. I just hate it.'

Immediately, she recognized the maudlin self-pity of a fatuity. She was familiar with the type, a number of her pious old ladies had blighted her nights and days by moaning in like vein.

'I'd love to see you, dear, but I'm rather busy at the moment, perhaps some time next week?'

She had never been ambitious herself, but then she had never carped about the absence of rewards a lack of ambition brought. Friends and family used to criticize her for wasting her talents. When she was thirteen she had been pressed to publish a sonnet she had written. She hadn't bothered, though she could remember it still.

> Shot through the eyes, the farmer's son comes home
> Whom war had done with. Never now again
> The little evil ways of death and pain
> Shall vex his heart with sorrow. He is come
> To mile on mile of downland. Through his hands
> The grasses run their warmth. The turtles' moaning,
> The threshers' whirr, these are his heritage,
> And scent and heat and music of his lands;
> And sight of these has passed beyond his owning.
> Here on the uplands, where alone he stands,

The sunlight on his blinded eyelids streaming,
He sees his wasted youth, his wasted age
Pass by, as ruined shadows through his dreaming.
'And ah,' he sighs, 'but life is hard to some.'

Francis lightly sprang from the bookcase to Bel's shoulder
and made squeaking noises. She realized that Bliss was still
talking.
' ... middle-aged. Nothing to believe in any longer. Worse,
unloved ... '
'Come this evening then. It'll have to be Cypriot sherry, I
won't have South African and I can't afford Spanish.'
The most wondrous thing about God was that He loved all
of His creation; moaners and flies just as much as saints and
penitents. She picked up her newspaper and read that five
million dollars in one-hundred dollar bills would weigh a
hundred and fifty-six pounds. Ah!

Bel unwrapped the bottle of medium-dry Cypriot sherry and
placed it on a tray with two glasses and a glass bowl of small
square cheese biscuits. The days were drawing in, she
switched on a light and with a handful of biscuits slowly walked
round her cramped bed-sitting-room surveying her pictures.
They gave her greater earthly pleasure than anything else. Her
favourite varied from time to time, but now she loved best one
of the Samuel Palmers. She gazed at it as if to enter it. A
smocked, straw-hatted farmer unyoked a massive, tranquil ox;
great fruits lolled from a sinewy tree and in the distance three
tumescent hills teemed with animals, corn and woods. In the
sky a thin crescent of a moon hung and illuminated all.
Bliss was late – so like him. She knew that friends and
family, particularly family, longed to know how she had come
by the pictures, but she could think of no good reason why
their curiosity should be satisfied. In fact she had bought them
from a young Englishman with money left her by the first and
only man she had ever loved. He was Captain Philip Brassman,
a stocky, much decorated soldier with a romantically shadowy
background in which he sheltered. Thirty years his junior, she
had been sixteen when she'd first met him and, as she had
written in her diary, she was 'Utterly dotty about him at first

glance, with a great hollow longing in my tummy.' Throughout their friendship he treated her with the greatest courtesy and the sweetest gentleness. He travelled much, for what purpose he never divulged. She never knew when she would see him, or for how long. And then one day, just before the outbreak of war, he went away and never came back. Later it was said that he'd gone over to the Russians, or that he'd been liquidated by them, or that he was a secret Zionist, or that he was a Nazi undercover agent. It was years before his will could be proved.

A constant concern of Bel's was to whom the pictures should pass on her death. She had no doubt that they were of national importance and, of course, extremely valuable. The Victoria and Albert, the Tate, the Ashmolean at Oxford would all be fit homes and all would be glad of them. Strictly speaking they were not part of the family heirlooms, and yet it saddened her to think that future generations of Lingfields would not treasure and delight in them as she did. At the moment, and her will had as many codicils as months of the year, they were left to Bliss. She had not told him, nor would she until she was sure she had made the right decision and she would not be sure until he showed some interest in them.

'Sorry I'm late.'

He was stooped and slightly pot-bellied, she had not seen him look so unwell. It was shocking because she had always thought of him as tall and spare.

'How's the family?'

When Bliss was a boy, after his father died, she had taken him to the seaside for short holidays. Ostensibly it was to give his mother peace and quiet to settle her husband's affairs, but really it was because Bel enjoyed being with her nephew and indulging him. They stayed at guesthouses at Deal and Walmer and Rottingdean. She played schoolboy games with him: digging channels in the clinging, sucking sand; teasing tiny crabs with twigs; combing the drift for treasure, ambergris and jewels. With delight she watched him demolishing great plates of bacon and eggs and sausages and beans. She had been proud of the colour that suffused his sweet distended cheeks.

'I don't see much of them. Briar occasionally comes round to cadge money and I haven't seen Crécy for weeks. By the way, where's Francis?'

14

'He's got a bit of a chill. I've put him to bed.'

Bliss stared at the floor. Bel tried to will him to look up, around, to catch sight of the pictures, say something about them, anything.

'D'you know, Bel, I really envy you. Here you are living in this insanitary dump ... '

Tact had never been Bliss's particular forte. She smiled forgivingly, though he wasn't looking at her, he was teasing his moustache.

' ... with no money and yet you're the only person I know who's happy.'

'What about all your rich, grand friends?'

'Not really. They're either getting divorced for the ump-teenth time, or being dried out, or being dunned. Toffy Lutyens told me the last time he'd been happy was when he'd been in a major car smash, that at least was exciting.'

'Sounds childish to me.'

'I can't really explain it, but all the things I used to enjoy, I now find desperately boring. Even gambling. I hardly do it now, and then only to make money.'

She thought, there is still hope for you. When he was a boy, she had surreptitiously lured him to Mass with the promise of chocolate cake and ice-cream afterwards. She could well understand how the anaemic service of morning prayer he daily suffered at school kindled no sparkle. And she knew that in the school holidays his parents were as likely to encourage him to enter a brothel as a church. On reflection, his father would have opted for the brothel. But in spite of her enticements, the miraculous transformation had not taken place. Bliss had merely expressed churlish boredom and stomach rumblings. Perhaps now, thirty years on, he was ripe.

'Give yourself some more sherry. Don't you feel something lacking in your life?'

The trouble was that, thirty years on, the Church was not what it was. What spiritual lure was there in the modern, emasculated goings-on?

'Everything, Bel. Everything.'

Unless she were to take him to a traditional Mass at the Oratory, or Farm Street?

'Our spirits need refreshment.'

15

'I hardly drink any longer.'

Perhaps it was already too late. She looked at him: he was decorous and, at the same time, shabby and sad.

'Bliss, you know you ought to have an occupation.'

He smiled, a transparently honest smile born of amused resignation. Rather engaging, like that of a hard-tried but endlessly patient child.

'I know that only too well. But not even the army would keep me on.'

'How about voluntary work, prison visiting, or hospitals, or geriatrics?'

'Yes, I suppose so.'

He was utterly unlike his father. Her brother might have been irascible and intolerant, but at least he had fire in his belly. Bliss's lassitude annoyed her.

'Well, it's up to you. Only you can pull your finger out.'

He flinched. She smiled inwardly, pleased both that she was able to shock him and that he was unable to conceal it. She relented; she would give him one more chance to enrich his life and salve his soul.

'Come to Mass with me?'

'Can I think about it?'

'Next Sunday?'

'I'm afraid the weekends are always bad for me. Next Sunday I'll be staying with the Delavaros.'

When he had gone, she went to her desk. In the centre drawer was a file marked: 'When I am dead'. Her fingers toyed with the handle.

Chapter Three

THROUGHOUT his life Bliss had despised whichever house he happened to be living in and mourned the loss of his previous home. So it was now. He sat in the basement kitchen, lamenting the degradation of a terrace house within walking distance of Victoria Station. He had been there for years, ever since his separation from Moyra. On the outside wall hung the two dead birds given him by Snipe. They gave the scanty area a spuriously opulent look.

He was waiting for his stockbroker to telephone. He liked to hear from Simon Montagu at least twice a day, preferably at ten and again at four – just to keep an ear to the ground. Simon was late. In spite of his name and looks Simon was about as truly Anglicized as anybody could be without being truly English. They had been to the same school; Simon had made the eleven, subsequently been elected to Boodle's and married Jackie Spencer-Howard's daughter. No outsider could hope for more than that. He'd probably seen the inside of a synagogue as many times as Bliss himself had. The front doorbell rang.

Bliss had forgotten that his son, Briar, had mentioned that he might drop round. Briar stood diffidently in the doorway, like a salesman with no expectation of a sale. He was a trimmer, lither version of his father. Outside his very tight black velvet trousers he wore an outsize shirt in the manner of a tunic. It reminded Bliss of a poster advertisement of the fifties or sixties in which a raunchy girl stood wearing nothing else. 'Looks better on a man.' Tootal, Van Heusen, Tern. It was funny, shirt manufacturers didn't seem to advertise any more. Staring at his sullenly-postured son, he idly wondered why.

17

'You look like a ballet dancer, Briar. Coffee, or would you like a drink?'

'Congratulations, Dad, that's the first time you've got my name right, off your own bat.'

Not long after her remarriage, Moyra had given his two children new Christian names. Crispian had become Briar and his daughter, Penelope, Crécy. Possibly some sort of swings and roundabouts gesture to the French. Sometimes, not always, as Briar had made out, he forgot.

'To what do I owe the pleasure?'

'Any gin about?'

They went upstairs to the drawing-room, scene of a vibrant exercise in interior decoration by an old flame now extinguished. Bliss blanched whenever he entered.

'Seen your sister?'

'That old scrubber, you must be joking.'

Bliss sipped a gin and tonic. Normally he eschewed gin in the middle of the day, but in the case of a confrontation with his son he found it palliative.

'So what are you up to?'

'I need some money, actually.'

He always did. His sister always did. They always did.

'Don't we all?'

'Mother thinks my allowance is pretty stingy.'

'Why doesn't she do something about it?'

'You are supposed to be my father.'

Whatever that meant.

'Fact is, I'm a bit pushed myself. Market's down.'

'Well, what do you suggest I do, rob a bank, go on the streets?'

Bliss had gone straight into the army from school. A stint in the Grenadiers – he'd enjoyed it, would have stayed on given the chance – but there was no point in suggesting it as a career to Briar.

'Shouldn't you get a job?'

'Speak for yourself. Anyway, haven't you heard, there are millions of unemployed?'

'What sort of things interest you? Maybe I could help.'

'I wouldn't mind Christie's, or the Church. All that dressing up and poncing around might be amusing.'

18

Notoriously, parents knew nothing of their children, but these ambitions of his son went beyond mere ignorance. Christie's was perhaps less astonishing than the quaintly expressed vocation to the priesthood, but Briar had never before expressed the slightest interest in matters aesthetic or spiritual. He looked at his son, expecting, hoping to see a smile of ridicule, but there was only a look of disdainful self-assurance.

'Well, I suppose that's a start. Have you made any inquiries?'

'God, not yet. I'm still considering what would be for the best.'

Cringing despair came to Bliss like an unwanted dog.

'I might be able to help with Christie's, I used to know Dicky D'Arcy. But you're on your own with the C. of E.'

The telephone rang.

'Bliss? Simon here. Sorry I haven't rung you earlier, it's a madhouse today. You remember the punt we had last week on Cleanands Mines?'

'Thirty thousand?'

'Right, I think it's time we got out.'

'Take our profit?'

'Not exactly. The fact is they're slipping. The whole market is on a downward trend.'

In the looking-glass over the mantelshelf Bliss saw his reflected son edging towards the drinks tray.

'What'll I lose?'

'Hang on a sec – get the old calculator out. You bought at three pounds fifty, they're now at two ninety-five, so you'll be down about seventeen thou.'

'God!'

'I'm sorry, Bliss. It shouldn't have happened. It's this damn business in South Africa, it's given everyone the jitters. Of course, if you wanted to, you could take them up.'

'What the hell with? I haven't got that sort of money hanging around.'

'Sell some of the stock you hold. The only drawback is that virtually everything is down.'

'Get rid of Cleanands then.'

'I think that's your best bet. Incidentally, we've weathered this sort of thing before, I wouldn't be too upset.'

19

'But seventeen thousand!'

'Well, the feeling in the market is that Cleanands will be out of the woods in a month. The South African tizzy will have died down by then. What I wonder is whether you want to do a call in the same amount. I could get you one at thirty pence to strike at three pounds and if the boys here are right and they go to three-ninety, you'll be out with an overall profit of three grand.'

'What'll that set me back?'

'Nine grand.'

'Oh God, do it.'

He put down the telephone. Briar was standing by the door looking unhealthily flushed.

'I've got to go now, Dad.'

'Look, Briar, I can let you have a cheque for a hundred if that'll help.'

The trouble with Simon was that he was more persuasive than Julian of Norwich in making one believe that all would be well. Every dandy chick fluttering about long before it had been hatched.

'That'll help a bit. By the way, Mother wants to see you.'

Where there were children a man could never be truly divorced from his former wife.

'Can't she ring me?'

'She said she wanted you to drop in for a drink tonight.'

'I can't. What's it all about?'

'Search me. What about tomorrow?'

'If I must.'

Outside it was drizzling. The pain in his back was as rhythmic as the beating of a drum. He wondered where he was going to find twenty-six thousand pounds in ten days. Briar was still by the door.

'Dad, you know those paintings of Bel's, reckon they're worth anything?'

There was no prior engagement that prevented Bliss from dropping in on Moyra, he simply wished to spend an evening alone with his worries and not to be at the beck and call of a woman who with her passion for manoeuvring others should have been a chess grandmaster.

20

He would make a list and then take a bath. For as long as he could remember he had made a daily list, it was a discipline that gave shape and purpose to his life.

Eggs
Milk
Bath
Bread
Money

There was something pleasantly rakish about bathing in the middle of the day. Having heard that mustard was a panacea, he liberally tipped some into the bath and without much faith eased his body into the steaming, tinted water. The heat dimmed his consciousness, fat drops of sweat slipped down his brow and stung his eyes. His fears lost their edge and from the particular became general. Women and money. They were the great principles of life, they were the sources of all suffering. One either had too much of one and too little of the other, or too little of the one and too much of the other. It was hell, to need things that by their very nature were pernicious. His observations impressed him, he would write them down, memorize them, drop them impromptu at the next dinner party. His hair was sticky, he would have to wash it. Mustard was no cure for backache. The telephone rang.

'Bel?'

Bliss stood chill-blasted by an open window, but too far from it to shut it. Wet patches on the carpet marked his way from the bathroom. Pools formed around his feet as he shivered.

'No, darling, it's Mother.'

'You got me out of the bath.'

'At this time of day? It's Clarry, this time he's done something appalling. You must come at once.'

21

Chapter Four

THE Dowager Lady Lingfield lived with her permanently confused brother Clarry – a diminutive fusion of Claude Henry – in Calcutta Court. Built between the wars, this mammoth pile had more in common with the tenement block it overshadowed at the back than its thickly carpeted foyer and resplendently uniformed porter might have suggested. In both the unappetizing aroma of cooking food seeped from under the doors and swirled down the interminable passages. In both the graffiti artist wielded penknife and paint-can to make his monosyllabic mark. In both the confined residents preserved a sullen anonymity.

Lady Lingfield's flat consisted of five small rooms that led off a passage, a microcosm of the labyrinth outside. Movement was hampered by grandiose pieces of protruding furniture. Full-length military portraits darkened the walls. Lady Lingfield intensely revered her chattels. She looked on them as part of her, as much as her skin and bones, and she believed that the removal of even one of them would diminish her. It was thirty years ago, but she still regretted the sale of her grand piano.

The size and awkwardness of the kitchen would have tried the patience of the most saintly chef, but – as Lady Lingfield admitted – she was a slave to prepared foods. Her store-cupboard was always well stocked with tins (including an inordinate number of pilchards in tomato sauce; she was apt to forget when shopping that she detested them) and her freezer groaned with frozen TV dinners. Long ago Clarry had mildly wondered why they never ate hot food or off plates. He'd understood entirely when it had been explained to him that the money they saved on electricity and washing-up liquid by eating straight from the tin or TV-dinner tray allowed them not to stint on gin.

Bliss entered Calcutta Court and as he took his first step on the yielding, deep pile of the maroon carpet in the foyer, felt his spirits sink. The porter, a plum-faced, bulbous man, moved slowly, resolutely towards him. He was a moaning toady. Bliss beat him to the lift. His mother's flat was on the third floor – too low to avoid the thunderous din of the traffic and not high enough to benefit from an aggrandizing view of the rooftops below.

He rang the bell and held his breath to keep out the warm fetid air. His mother opened the door and regarded him with a mixture of surprise and impatience. She was a stout, bloom-complexioned woman. Clarry stood behind her, cherubic and silken-skinned with a look of happy expectancy. He wore, as usual, a dapper double-breasted blue pinstriped suit, and a tie that mistakenly suggested some regimental or old-school connection.

'Clarry's been looking forward to seeing you. I told him he could have one drink with us.'

She spoke of her brother as if he were not there.

'Then he must go to his room. I want a proper talk with you, in private.'

Clarry beamed and poured gin into three tiny tumblers decorated with coloured sailing-boats. He looked at his nephew mischievously.

'Bliss, old gobemouche, what's the difference between a goatsucker and a nightjar?'

'Clarry, that's enough of that nonsense. I've told you before I won't have it in front of guests.'

Lady Lingfield eyed her brother severely and sipped her gin. She always sipped. Momentarily abashed, Clarry gazed at his plaid slippers. His sister had always been censorious of his pastimes. For ages he had filled the long hours between his tinned lunch and the start of children's television in perusing a dictionary he had discovered in his sister's bookcase. When-ever he came across an odd word he would note it, and when he had culled enough words to make a short and nonsensical sentence, he would devise one so that he might later surprise and delight friends and visitors to his sister's home. This, and his major undertaking of counting up to a million, were his principal pleasures and commitments in life.

'I give up.'

Clarry's head shot up, the prodigal shriven.

'There's no difference; they're both the same.'

'How's the counting?'

Clarry pulled four shabby pieces of paper from his pocket. They were respectively headed: hundred thousands, ten thousands, thousands and hundreds, and were marked with neat notations. He pored over them with unconcealed absorption, his lips nimbly moving, making soft smacking noises. When he looked up he was pink with pride.

'Two hundred and eighty-four thousand, three hundred and fifty. And that's only taken four months.'

'Clarry, that's enough! Off to your room. And, Bliss, you shouldn't encourage him.'

Clarry gathered up his tally-sheets and stumped from the room. Lady Lingfield waited, an ear cocked and then bent close to her son and whispered.

'He's become such a worry. He'll have to be put in a home soon, though where we'll find the money – and the nice ones are so expensive.'

Bliss edged away from his mother. In the circumstances he found her use of the first person plural threatening. Sparks of gin flew from her lips as she continued.

'If only we still had Lingfield Place, it was madness to sell it. Eight thousand pounds!'

She sighed. Lingfield Place, the family seat, a pleasant Regency house standing in parkland had been sold with the home farm on the death of Bliss's father. Bliss had not been ten at the time. He had long suspected that his mother somehow blamed him.

'We could all have lived there. So good for the children and you could have busied yourself with the farm. You and Moyra'd still be together. How I wish I could turn the clock back. You know I had strong forebodings that morning he set off for London.'

This was an oft-aired tale of regret. Bliss's father, a retired colonel in the Guards who had spent the war years storming through the Near East and Europe tussling with the Axis foe, had been knocked down and killed by a charabanc of Japanese tourists outside Westminster Abbey. He was on his way there for a memorial service.

'Clarry used to be just silly, but now ... '

Bliss poured more gin and looked anxiously round the room for any visible signs of what his uncle had become. On a table copies of health food magazines lay neatly piled. But these he knew were his mother's, she read them as an act of penance for her own diet.

'I've had to cancel my Harrods account.'

'Why?'

Bliss immediately recognized that this indicated something serious, like the loss of Jerusalem for the Jews or his punt on Cleanands Mines.

'Clarry's been ordering things on my account.'

It seemed innocent enough.

'So?'

'But hundreds of things. Dozens of Korans, a gross of surgical gloves, scores of hideous porcelain shepherdesses and sacks and sacks of carrots.'

The door flew open and there stood Clarry dressed as before but with a large carrot immodestly sticking out of his trousers. Nobody spoke and then Clarry with deliberation looked down, feigned shock and with a pair of scissors severed the offending vegetable. As it fell he boomed at them both.

'Kava and poontang manumit me.'

Chapter Five

LINGFIELD Place was now the home of the Little Sisters of St Luke, a community dedicated to prayer for the mortally ill. By contemporary standards it was quite a large and flourishing order.

'What we need is a miracle and if we can't have a real one I'm all for fabricating one.'

It was the Mother Superior, Euberta, a jovial overweight woman who spoke. She was seated at her desk going through the post with her secretary and confidante Sister Beatrice.

'Really, Reverend Mother, what a thing to say. And why do we need a miracle?'

'More money, more vocations, to halt the country's slide to heathenism. Miracles always prompt these things.'

The house and the land had changed since the Lingfield family had lived there, though they would not have found it unrecognizable. Most of the oaks in the park had gone and the park itself had shrunk. Part of it had been sold to a developer who had built an estate of neo-Georgian town houses, each one with its own brass carriage lamp by the front door and two-car garage at the side. The home farm was now owned by a London investment company. It was intensively farmed, the woods and most of the hedges had been uprooted.

'And what sort of miracle were you planning on?'

'Oh, nothing too sensational.'

The exterior of the house lacked its former symmetry, several prefabricated huts had sprouted from one wing. These were used by the community for the manufacture of devotional objects and for the preparation of home-made jams and pâtés marketed under the name 'St Luke's Lucullan Delights'. Without the sale of these products there would have been no community.

Inside the house proper, austerity was the order in all but the guest-rooms. The guest bathroom walls were lined from floor to ceiling with deftly painted Dutch tiles, blue on white. As a child Bliss had been fascinated by the pattern of tiny windmills, castles, skaters, fisherfolk. The bedrooms still had the old carpets, curtains and pretty, faded French floral wallpaper and, though dowdy, were invitingly comfortable. The chapel, once the Lingfield dining-room and daringly art nouveau, was now – in line with current ecclesiastical fashion – severely unadorned. Mother Superior's office overlooked the extant rose-garden and, beyond the ha-ha and overgrown orchard, to a wooded hill that crouched like an obedient dog.

'Our business is to pray for the dying, just suppose our prayers brought back somebody, preferably well known, from the very brink of death. You know how the media love such things.'

'It would be wonderful, Reverend Mother, but you mentioned fabricating one.'

'How often have I told you, my child, that God moves in a mysterious way.'

Chapter Six

'**Y**OU know Bliss is dropping in for a drink.'

Terrick House was a fine, red-bricked Queen Anne mansion set not far back from the river in Chelsea. It was the London home of the Earl of Terrick and his wife Moyra. The house had been bought and renamed in the twenties after a rather opaque business transaction, though the family never went to great pains to disabuse those who believed it had been Terrick since time immemorial.

'Did you hear? Bliss is coming round.'

Moyra was ten years younger than her husband but looked much younger. Tall, with dark hair, she had purpley-blue eyes and a hurt expression that elicited sympathy from people who did not know her well. She maintained that she was uninterested in fashion but was always handsomely dressed in a simple, classical style. Now, standing in the doorway of the study, she wore a light grey wool suit, a pale blue silk shirt and, round her neck, four rows of pearls.

'Actually I'd forgotten. What for?'

Teddy-Bear, as the Earl was affectionately known to his family and close friends, still found Bliss's presence uncomfortable even though he'd been married to Moyra for eight years. With Bliss in the same room he felt like a sweet-stealing boy caught with the evidence in his mouth. Had the circumstances been different he thought they might have been friends. Teddy-Bear was a mild man whose pleasures, when he was allowed them, were simple. He liked the country and shooting and fishing, but since his marriage he found that he spent more and more time in London where he was generally at a loss to know what to do.

'It's about the children. Bliss is simply not pulling his weight.'

28

'Oh!'

'He's coming after six. Shall we have drinks here or in the drawing-room?'

'Perhaps the drawing-room. Do I have to be there?'

'Of course. I think here would be better. I'll tell Taylor.'

She went away. He was quite glad that she had gone. He turned back to *Country Life*. Half looking at the pictures and half looking out of the window at the walled garden, he mused that autumn was not such a bad season. The garden, large for a London house, had a small orchard at the far end and the leaves were beginning to turn. The roses in the circular bed in the centre of the lawn were still magnificent. Barry, a young lad from Battersea was growing into an accomplished gardener. From time to time he could see Barry's head bobbing up above the yew hedge that hid the vegetable-garden. He was probably digging up potatoes.

Teddy-Bear caught sight of his reflection in a window-pane and looked away in disgust. Some years ago he had suffered a minor stroke that had left the right side of his body partly paralysed. Half of his face perpetually bore an infernal grin.

Bliss hailed a taxi. Some months ago when driving he'd had a skirmish with a pram-pushing black woman and, *force majeure*, he no longer drove. His had been a terrible day. He'd rung Simon, who'd told him that the sooner he found twenty-six thousand the better as the market was crumbling.

'Obviously, the way things are, whatever you do you're bound to make some capital loss, but just think of it as a temporary set-back. And don't forget any loss can be put down as an accumulative capital minus against any future gain.'

Listening to Simon, Bliss had felt quite happy, almost wealthy, but now watching the mounting figures on the meter he only knew that he was having to sell twenty-six thousand pounds worth of his precious stock. His life blood. And his back pained him.

The taxi pulled up. In years gone by he had trembled on having to confront his ex-wife – now he merely dreaded having to listen to her.

'Hello, Bliss. She says we ought to have drinks in the study.'

Bliss had never had anything against Teddy-Bear except his

nickname and his wealth. He wondered if the worst came to the worst, whether he could touch him. They walked down a broad, portrait-lined corridor. Three hundred years of family history; the ancestral characteristic, the upturned button nose, variously recorded by Kneller, Romney, Sargent, Sutherland (a bold choice). Bliss slowed his pace to allow for his host's dragging limp.

'Planning on going away this winter, Bliss?'

'If I can afford the fare, I thought I might take the Underground to Gloucester Road.'

'Ha! that's a good one. I must remember that.'

The study was at the end of the house, Bliss had been in it before. They trudged on. It was the most absurd anachronism: a palatial country house in the middle of London in the age of the chip and the clone.

'How about you?'

'We've got the first shoot on the tenth so I'll pop down to Ramillies a few days before – if Moyra will let me.'

Teddy-Bear made a soft rumbling sound that might have been a sad laugh.

'We must get you down, Bliss. One of these days.'

Ramillies, a great stone monument to power and position built in the early eighteenth century, was Teddy-Bear's seat. Surrounded by thousands of acres of Gloucestershire farmland the whole estate was enclosed by a lofty wall that was known locally, not entirely good-naturedly, as the Great Wall. Bliss had driven past the main gate but had never been inside. On a few, deliberately confusing days of the year (the first Friday and fourth Thursday of alternate months) it was open to the public.

'Hello, darling.'

It was typical of Moyra that, having assiduously avoided using that endearment during the years of her marriage to Bliss, she should now use it whenever they met. With her back to the window she was framed by the last of the day's sunlight. It might have been his imagination but he suspected she would enjoy teasing him astray.

'So good of you to come, Bliss darling, when you're so busy. You must be working frightfully hard at something, you look so exhausted. Teddy-Bear, aren't you going to offer our guest a drink?'

Moyra's husband started like a nervous horse and fled to the drinks-tray.

'Darling, you know me, I don't beat about the bush, I want to talk about our children.'

When Bliss was four, he had been made by his mother, much against his will, to go on a Sunday-School treat to the seaside. He had not known the other children well and had spent the day as far as possible away from them. Just before they were all due to return home he had fallen into the water and soaked himself and his clothes. The only person who had brought a change of clothing was a big boisterous, ten-year-old girl whose budding sensuality had on occasions agitated him before. It was her shorts and blouse that he had had to change into. Moyra was capable of engendering the same shameful humiliation that he'd first felt all those years ago. He took the tumbler of whisky from Teddy-Bear's trembly hand.

'You see, darling, I don't want to get shirty or anything, but I really don't think you're doing your whack.'

'I thought Briar looked very well the other day. Will I see Crécy tonight?'

Bliss congratulated himself on remembering his children's relatively new names. When Crécy had been Penelope she had crawled into his bed one Sunday morning and lain with her head by his on the pillow, her toes just reaching his stomach. It was the only time in his life that anyone had said, without prompting or expectation of reward, that she loved him. Now he suspected a contempt for him had been successfully instilled into her.

'My God! That's it in a nutshell; you take so much interest in your daughter you don't even know where she's living.'

'Where is she?'

'She hasn't been here for months. She's living with a black in Whitechapel or a white in Blackfriars, a ghastly creature called Quinn or something. Teddy-Bear, be an angel and give me a refill.'

Bliss was uncomfortably warm, it must have been the whisky. He ran a finger between his collar and neck.

'And money! How on earth do you expect them to survive on the pittances you give them. It's not surprising Crécy looks like an orphan and acts like a whore.'

31

She was like a dynamo, her anger burning brighter as she accelerated her argument. Out of the corner of an eye Bliss could see Teddy-Bear gazing into the garden, seeking a refuge for his embarrassment.

' ... if it weren't for the little Teddy-Bear and I ... '

Bliss thought of the Codex Terrick, the rolling Gloucestershire acres, the Ramillies service. Envy was a more painful chastiser than jealousy.

' ... our outgoings are enormous and you only have the upkeep of a tiny terrace house.'

He was hot and rather dizzy. Everything in the room seemed suddenly far away. Moyra's voice was no longer piercing but remote. The sensation reminded him of a similar experience at his prep school. Then the school matron had told him it was a symptom of growing up and given him an aspirin. God, he couldn't still be growing up. He struggled to breathe. He tried to put his glass down, everything was so distant, and heard a dull breaking sound. Then from far away he saw the intricately patterned carpet racing towards him.

Infinity was a box with neither top, nor bottom, nor sides. It was quite simple, there were many infinities, each presided over by its own creator-god, each subject to its own natural and supernatural laws. It was like coming round from an anaesthetic.

Bliss opened his eyes and looked up to an elaborate chinoiserie ceiling. He hadn't noticed it before. He was lying on the floor. There were spatters of blood on his white shirt. Above him loomed Moyra and Teddy-Bear and, surprisingly, Crécy. He wanted someone to account for his daughter's presence but he could not speak. The three of them were staring at him with a mixture of bewilderment and disapproval.

Chapter Seven

'IT'S just not fair.'

'I know, darling, I know.'

None of Briar's friends would have thought of him as concerned but he was tormented now by a worry that was as insistent as a tumour on the brain. It wrought havoc with his hours of sleep, it blighted his daytime pleasures. He sat on the grass in the park discussing it with Travers, his closest friend and sole confidant.

Travers scooped a blade of blond hair back from his brow. He described himself as a commission man. He had the amoral serenity of a Botticelli angel past its prime. Whenever his wealthy friends or acquaintances wished to buy or sell valuables (yachts, jewellery, estates, paintings, anything, provided it was expensive), he found the best market and negotiated the transaction. For his pains, which were rarely excruciating, he took a modest ten per cent (so he claimed) of the price paid. As a result he was now richer than most of his acquaintances and almost as rich as some of his friends.

'Travers, you know me inside out. I'm simply not the stuff of a nine-to-five man ... '

Briar looked sulky and impetuously plucked blades of grass.

'I've got nothing against people who can do it. But, God, the very thought of having to spend the day listening to their bourgeois sentiments and then having to endure their sweaty bodies on the Underground.'

'I thought you liked sweaty bodies, but exactly what expectations have you got?'

Briar left the grass alone and stared bewilderedly at his friend.

'That's it. None – absolutely none.'

33

'Come on, darling, don't be melancholy. What about your father?'

'He's frittered practically everything away. He thinks only of himself.'

'And your mother?'

'Don't think she's got much of her own, she just bleeds Teddy-Bear dry.'

'What about him?'

'His stuff's all entailed. Anything he can keep from my mother he ploughs back into Ramillies. And then there's some bloody second cousin in Alberta.'

'No grannies, aunts, uncles or benighted old queens?'

Briar dismally shook his head and then abruptly stopped. His eyes glimmered with distant hope.

'There is Bel, my great-aunt, she lives in a tenement block with her monkey ... '

'Doesn't sound very propitious.'

It was nearly lunchtime. Travers wanted the discussion to close. He was fond, inordinately fond of darling Briar, but he didn't like sitting on grass and he disliked his friends being needy. The Ritz was not far off, he thought of the scintillating gin fizz he might have been enjoying there.

'She has some pictures.'

'What sort of pictures?'

Travers envisaged the walls of the tenement flat enhanced with passe-partout-framed reproductions culled from Christmas numbers of the *Illustrated London News*.

'Oh, country scenes, that sort of thing. You know, dark, boring and Victorian.'

'Are they paintings?'

'Of course, water-colours, oils. She's very proud of them actually.'

No doubt daintily painted by the great-aunt's great-aunt.

'Are they by anybody in particular?'

Briar looked brittly annoyed as if he suspected Travers of ridiculing him.

'Obviously, I wouldn't have mentioned them otherwise.'

Briar pouted and returned to grass-plucking. In the early days of their friendship his pettishness had been an engaging part of his vulnerability; now it was tedious and invidious.

34

'Well, who?'

'Oh, Blake, Farmer, people like that.'

'You don't mean Palmer?'

'Probably, I've never been good at names.'

Travers' interest secured, Briar celebrated modestly; he yawned, sucked a daisy, dismembered another. It was a fair display of studied indifference.

'How many are there?'

'Oh, I don't know, you're so quantitative, less than a dozen. They're awfully grimy and dull.'

'Who is she leaving them to?'

'She always said she'd leave them to anyone who showed some interest in them.'

'How old is she?'

'Seventies, I suppose, but she's pretty fit.'

'Let's go and have a drink.'

Travers was on his feet, he stretched out a hand and lightly drew Briar up from the grass.

'What's on your mind, Travers?'

Feigning apathy to a friend's enthusiasm was one of Briar's simple pleasures, but the time for that had now passed. In the end Travers' schemes were always irresistibly infectious; all the more so in this case when Briar himself was the object of them.

'Just a thought.'

Travers had the contented look of a man who, if he did not see the answer, saw that there might be one.

'Just how much did you say you needed a year to live on?'

'I could scrape by on twenty thou.'

'And how many paintings?'

'Nine actually. Two Blakes, four Palmers and three Calverts. The Palmers and Calverts are all Shoreham period.'

'You're pretty knowledgeable really, darling.'

They laughed together.

'Briar, what I'm going to tell you you must treat in absolutely the strictest confidence. Do you understand? By the way, are you desperately fond of your great-aunt?'

'Not exactly desperately.'

Caught in a sunbeam they made a pretty pair as they jauntily crossed the park. People in scattered deck-chairs or lying on the grass enjoying the unseasonable warmth looked up to watch them pass. Briar in his spotless white and Travers in a velvet suit of Oxford blue. One raven, one blond.

'Some years ago a friend of my father's, obviously I can't tell you his name, was threatened with financial disaster. He tried everything but finally realized that the only thing that would save him, his family and his business was his mother's estate which – bar a few small bequests – was left entirely to him. She was old, had had a full and happy life and had only senility to look forward to. None the less the idea of speeding up her departure appalled him. In despair he appealed to my father for advice.'

A couple came towards them. The man, tall, robust and a victim of thalidomide, held one of his girlfriend's fingers in the three of his that jutted from his shoulder. Neither Briar nor Travers noticed them.

'He and my father argued about it for days. In the end my father persuaded him that he had no option and that any remorse he might feel would be nothing compared to the break-up of his family life.'

They came to Piccadilly. A haze of fumes hovered over the jammed traffic. From Hyde Park Corner came the impotent dissonance of car horns.

'What happened?'

'He did what he had to do, very swiftly and very humanely. He said afterwards that his mother couldn't possibly have had time to know what was happening to her. And this is the most important point, he told my father he'd never suffered the slightest remorse.'

'Is he still alive?'

'He's done remarkably well, raised a large and happy family. Funnily enough I sold him a Degas a few months ago.'

A doorman in blue and gold hat and coat greeted them.

'It's only an idea, darling. Anyway here we are. I'm for a gin fizz, how about you?'

Chapter Eight

'BLISS, you're looking more cadaverous than ever, darling. When are you going to cover us both with your shroud?'

Hermione, third wife of the Count de Pereira, for whom the zip was allegedly invented, was still sufficiently beautiful to get away with such archness.

'Forget it – I'm sterile or impotent or both.'

They were fellow dinner guests of a miraculously wealthy Lebanese couple intent on reaching the very pinnacles of international society. Among the other guests at their Eaton Square apartment were a German industrialist prince; Caix, the fashionable interior designer; a duchess who took photographs and, curiously, a man called Gwynn who painted.

'Darling, what's happened to you? You were always morbid, but never macabre.'

Gwynn, who had only been invited that morning, sat on Hermione's other side. He was rubbery-skinned, thin-haired and entirely ambivalent by nature. Next to him was the host's aunt; an elegant, antiquated lady who was deaf. So far Gwynn had hardly spoken. He knew precisely why he had been invited. He didn't mind, he was pleased to be there, he wasn't proud.

Hermione leant towards Bliss, the ends of her hair trailed in his *koulibiatschki*.

'Bliss, who is that crashing bore on my right?'

Bliss cursorily inspected Gwynn.

'No idea, never seen the fellow before.'

But Gwynn knew Bliss. He had not forgotten him. They had been together at school and being junior by several years Gwynn had suffered variously at Bliss's hands.

'He only opens his mouth to plug it with food. Darling, I've got the most frightfully good idea, Perry and I are going to Kenya next month, why don't you come with us?'

Gwynn, who had overheard everything, smiled to himself. Since his schooldays he had not been able to resist a sycophantic admiration for those he considered his superiors. At school he had idolized Bliss. Bliss was a baron, Bliss was rangy and handsome, Bliss was clever, Bliss disparaged games but excelled at them, Bliss was universally popular. Whereas he, Gwynn, the earnest son of a diligent solicitor, was squat and plain, dull at work, dismal at games and not so much unpopular as ignored. While Gwynn had been tucking into baked beans on toast for tea, Bliss had been eating pheasant.

With the arrival of fruit on the table the conversation became general – or, rather, was dominated by the German prince and the host. His aunt with total incomprehension looked round the company and dispensed encouraging smiles.

Shortly after the appearance of coffee, Gwynn followed Bliss from the dining-room. When he opened the lavatory door Bliss, his tie and collar loosened, was leaning over the hand-basin spitting.

'I don't suppose you remember me, but we were at school together.'

Bliss said nothing, didn't even look up, but spat again into the basin.

'We were in the same house, though you were a few years older than me.'

As if only at school did time exist. Bliss blew his nose in his left hand and then rinsed it under the tap. There were scummy traces of red in the basin.

'I think for a short time you were my fag master. Aren't you feeling well?'

Bliss had beaten him once, but he did not think it appropriate to mention it. There had been worse, too.

'It probably won't mean anything to you, but my name is Gwynn.'

Bliss looked up from the basin and regarded him with ferocious contempt. Gwynn was so nonplussed he could think of nothing to say, instead he concerned himself with shaking his member dry. Bliss's face between his cheeks and his chin was dappled with blood. Gwynn felt he must say something.

'Do you do this often?'

Bliss returned to the basin and smacked handfuls of water about his face. He did not speak.

'Perhaps you ought to see a doctor.'

By the time Gwynn returned to the party the other guests had formed new conversational groups. Hermione was animatedly discussing euthanasia with the German prince. Gwynn did not stay long, he wanted to get home. It gave him a perverse pleasure that the girl awaiting him there was Bliss's daughter.

Chapter Nine

THE doctor's waiting-room smelled of damp dogs. Lassitude and resignation hung heavily in the humid air. On the walls there were black and white photographs of sporting groups and admonitions not to smoke. On a low, palely-varnished table lay piles of limp magazines. Not one of them was more than a few months old. Two silent, plaster-complexioned women (they might have been sisters) and a fidgety, coughing man sat on the bench ahead of Bliss. A sniffling boy with oyster-snotty nose roamed the room aimlessly. Bliss picked up a magazine; it felt moist, as if it had been left outside overnight – or worse. Bangkok, he learnt, with its gilded massage girls and temples was sinking into the sea. Bliss was surprised; he had not known that Bangkok was anywhere near the sea. Over the page he was informed that the proportion of privately educated children was greater in France and America than in Britain. That, surely, could not be true.

'Next, please.'

Bliss looked up; he was alone now with the coughing man. The summons was chilling, its brusque indifference reminiscent of the brutal discipline of his schooldays. He and another shivering boy were standing outside the prefects' room waiting for the summons, 'Next, please.' And then: accusation, inquisition, confession, judgment and inescapable punishment. One year the technique of terror had been refined to perfection. Every night after prayers when the boys had gone to their rooms the junior prefect would sweep through the house thrashing the doors, walls and banisters with his cane, seeking out the guilty. Every night Bliss would sit on the edge of his chair, never sure he was not culpable, paralysed with fear, waiting and praying for the angry torment to pass him by.

40

'Next, please.'

The consulting-room was a contrast to the waiting-room. At one end a large bay window looked out on to a lush garden. The walls were upholstered in strawberry-blonde brushed suede and were hung with large, meretricious still lifes after the Dutch manner. At a great table of tubular chrome and plate-glass sat the doctor, busily writing. An athletic-looking woman in white asked Bliss his name and told him to sit down. The chair, facing the doctor, was slightly springy and did not inspire a feeling of ease.

'And what's your trouble?'

There was a whiff of the Antipodes in the doctor's voice, and a hint of irritation, as if he suspected his time was about to be wasted.

'I have a pain in my back.'

He was about Bliss's age and, though seated, was clearly an exceptionally short man. Perhaps to compensate for his height his head was crowned with a high dome. He looked like a white Mekon.

'We all have those from time to time.'

The athletic woman handed the doctor a brown envelope. He removed a card from it and instantly his manner changed. He smiled, revealing a shambles of teeth, and when he spoke it was with the warmth that a host reserves for an honoured guest.

'Ah, Lord Lingfield. Your first visit, I see. You're the sort of patient every doctor prays for.'

Bliss winced at the ebullience. The woman stood behind the doctor. She, too, was rippling with smiles.

'Now, Lord Lingfield, I imagine you would like to be a private patient.'

'No actually.'

The enthusiasm wilted a fraction.

'How very egalitarian of you.'

Bliss decided that nothing would be gained by explaining that his preference for the National Health Service was based on fear of his bank manager and not respect for Bevan.

'We'd better take a look at you on the couch. Slip off your jacket and shirt.'

The couch was very hard. Bliss found it impossible to rest

his head comfortably. He wished the woman would depart and that the stethoscope was not so cold.

'Breathe in deeply, please. Tell me where the pain is.'

'The other side.'

The cool fingers searched and prodded.

'Breathe in, Lord Lingfield, please.'

The voice lingered on the name.

'There?'

'No, lower. Just below the shoulder-blade.'

The fingers pressed inquisitively, almost viciously.

'There?'

'Yes.'

'I see. Breathe in again ... and out. Yes, I see. You may get dressed.'

To his surprise Bliss realized his hands were quivering, it was hard to button up his shirt. The same thing had happened to him when a schoolboy, changing after football matches on the icy Sussex coast.

'When you're ready, Lord Lingfield, there are one or two questions I'd like to ask.'

The doctor had returned to his desk and sat there rubbing his hands together and beaming like a man who had enjoyed a noble feast. In front of him lay a pad and pen.

'Do you smoke, Lord Lingfield?'

'No, thank you.'

The doctor laughed good-naturedly.

'I mean are you in the habit of smoking?'

'No.'

'Were you ever a smoker?'

'Not really.'

Bliss wondered why the man was so obsessed with smoking when all he'd come to see him about was a pain in the back. It was typical of doctors: at school there had been one known as 'Bags-down' Wilberforce. Whatever a boy's complaint was, broken thumb or nosebleed, Wilberforce would tell him to take his bags down.

'Do you drink much?'

'Occasionally, not very often.'

'When does the pain hurt most?'

'When I try to take a deep breath.'

42

'Do you get short of breath easily?'

Bliss laughed. The doctor only smiled in response and scribbled on his pad.

'Well, actually yes. Galloping middle age, I suppose.'

The woman in white was standing by the bay window. Sometimes she appeared to be listening to what was going on, sometimes she gazed absent-mindedly into the garden.

'Can you think of anything else amiss, Lord Lingfield?'

'Amiss' struck Bliss as a strange word in the circumstances. The woman remained where she was. It was worse than confession, at least Catholics only had to divulge their secrets to one person.

'My night life is not what it was.'

'You're not sleeping well?'

'No, my night life when I'm awake.'

The doctor went 'Ah!' and smiled conspiratorially. More scribblings.

'Nothing else unusual?'

Bliss hesitated, his eyes scanned the objects on the table. It seemed rather wet to mention the blood-spitting, after all he'd only come to see the man about his back. There wasn't much on the table: pen-tray, blotter, empty scummy coffee cup.

'Well, there's the blood. I occasionally spit up blood.'

'Much?'

Bliss scratched his moustache and tried, rather ineffectually, to chuckle.

'I don't bleed to death, but it can be awkward socially.'

The doctor pushed his chair away from the table and crossed his short legs over, a gesture that habitually signalled the final stage of the consultation.

'I'd like you to see someone else, Lord Lingfield.'

'You can't give me a prescription?'

'Well, I think it would be better at this moment in time if you saw a specialist. Just so we know exactly where we stand.'

'OK.'

'You're sure you don't want to be a private patient, it speeds things up. You're not on BUPA or anything?'

'No. I don't mind waiting.'

'The man I want you to see is Dr Israel. He's at the Brompton Hospital. A very fine diagnostician.'

43

'Sounds Jewish.'
'He is. You've no objections?'
Bliss flushed.

The doctor stood up and stretched. He stuck his chest out defiantly and turned to the woman in white.

'That proves what I've always maintained about British aristos.'

'What's that?'

'They're heroic stoics.'

'Or too damn dumb to know when they've had it.'

'Ah well, let's shut up shop – it's time for a gin.'

Chapter Ten

MOYRA Terrick was wrong about Gwynn; he lived neither in Blackfriars nor Whitechapel. The colour of his skin was white.

South of the Euston Road and north of Bloomsbury a few wretched streets defied the times. The houses, dwarfed and hemmed in by a monolithic hospital, the Post Office Tower and a bright, new council estate – as yet only superficially vandalized – lingered on with crumbling stucco and flaking paintwork. On a corner, a Welsh dairy, still with marble counter, served a diminishing clientele with an ever diminishing stock. Elsewhere there were East Mediterranean restaurants with insubstantial Doric columns and grandiose names: 'Great Alexander's Palace', 'Plato's Pizza Parlour'. There were faded placards stuck in cracked windows offering bespoke tailoring and shoes, and there were dog-eared invitations to brief encounters. In one such house, on the ground floor, lived Gwynn.

Known at the art school where he taught as the shaman, Gwynn had enticed and enjoyed many a silly and susceptible girl in what he called his studio. It was, in fact, merely a largish room of great squalor. Leading off from it were two other rooms. One served as an insanitary kitchen and lavatory, the other as a soiled bedroom. Both were without windows and airless. Gwynn took a perverse pride in his accumulated filth. In his studio, whose walls and bare floors were littered with pictures, a bohemian disorder had been cunningly contrived. Crécy adored it. It was so diametrically (a new word – picked up from Gwynn) unlike anything she'd known before and so authentic.

She lay on a disembowelled sofa eating a peanut-butter

sandwich, watching Gwynn roll a cigarette. The second-hand, muslin wedding dress she wore was no longer immaculately white. She let her head rest on the sofa arm and shut her eyes to savour and convince herself of her happiness.

Neither of her parents had understood her, nor she them. Life with Teddy-Bear and Mummy had been so ordinary and predictable, so corruptingly affluent. And before that, when her parents had been married, it had been crabby and discontentedly materialistic. 'Look at the mess you've made of the carpet. And it was only laid last year.' She was amazed she hadn't gone mad, ravaged their homes and smashed their stupid, precious possessions. It was as if she had spent all her life waiting in a gilded but dark and clammy room for a refreshing storm to break. Thanks to God and Gwynn it had. True, her mother had cut off her allowance, but that was a trifling price to pay for a life free of bourgeois obsessions and obligations. She opened her eyes. Gwynn was lighting his thin and battered cigarette from a fearsome flame that shot forth from a severed gas pipe. He blew a dense, bluish cloud of smoke in her direction. She basked in it.

'Crécy, do you mind about the money?'

'I don't, if you don't.'

Her wiry, dark golden hair and deep blue, apparently myopic eyes had caught his attention the day she joined his drawing class at the Byam Shaw. Her hair was extraordinarily thick for a blonde and at the time he had idly wondered whether it was naturally fair. Even he had been surprised by the speed with which the speculation had been corroborated.

'If only teaching paid better. I had hoped we might go to Tuscany.'

'Couldn't you have an exhibition?'

He smiled at her with fatherly condescension.

'It's not quite that easy.'

'I don't know why. I think you're brilliant, and you're so varied.'

She left the sofa and slowly wandered round the room, raptly examining her teacher and lover's works. Though she might be innocent of the machinations of the art world she was in one respect unassailably correct: Gwynn's work showed catholicity of influences. There was an interior with a sunbathed woman seated at a food-laden table that the unenlightened might have mistaken for a Bonnard, a pencil drawing of Jerusalem that smacked heavily of Edward Lear, a severe composition deeply indebted to Mondrian. And more.

'What did your mother say?'

'Oh, she was adamant.'

The alacrity with which Crécy had accepted his invitation to private lessons was matched only by the promptness with which, uninvited, she had moved in. He had realized it was to be on a semi-permanent basis when she had returned from a local street market with an armful of plastic bags stuffed with a motley of second-hand clothes. He had asked her why she had not collected her own clothes from home and she had disconcertingly replied that she had been reborn.

'Honestly, darling, don't worry, we'll be all right, I'll get my friends to commission you to do their portraits. If we're really pushed I can always become a tart.'

Gwynn smiled weakly and murmured 'Christ' to himself. She made him feel his age. He was flattered by her infatuation and depressed by it too. At the beginning he had doubted its durability but then, as it persisted, it occurred to him that it might provide an escape from the monotony of teaching and domestic squalor. In moments of euphoria he pictured them living together in a Tuscan farmhouse: while she contentedly fed the hens and tended the vines he would be painting dazzling landscapes and drawing like an angel. At night under the glittering blue dome of the sky he would make love to her on the cool grass with the furious zeal of a teenager.

'I can't tell you, darling, what it means to me to be really living. I wouldn't change this for the world.'

With outstretched arms and open hands Crécy indicated what she wouldn't change for all the world. There was a suggestion of the Pantocrator. Gwynn couldn't bear to look at her. He wondered how long it would be before she tired of slumming.

'You can't imagine what totally shallow lives Mummy and her friends lead. Daddy too.'

One day she would slip away, leaving behind her tatty, second-hand clothes crumpled in their plastic bags, to return to her proper station in life and to select a superficial but suitable mate. Perhaps he would meet her again at one of her less conventional friends' parties and perhaps she would not trouble to remember him.

'Do you know, it always amazes me that you and Daddy could have been at school together? Were you friends?'

He didn't like her phrasing, it implied a gulf and that she was fully aware on which side she and her father stood.

'Not exactly.'

Her father had been one of a gang of older boys who had chased him down a passage into the cul-de-sac of his room.

'Didn't you like him?'

'Not much. He helped to debag me once.'

She put her hand to her mouth but couldn't suppress a screech of laughter. The noise reminded him of everything he'd enviously despised all those years ago at school.

'What happened?'

She was as expectantly excited as a child watching the wild animals at a circus angrily slinking down the caged tunnel to the arena.

'Do you really want to know?'

He remembered it well. There had been about five of them. They had stood around his half-naked body gawping.

'Of course I do.'

Two of them had pulled his legs apart and then Lingfield had fondled him. He remembered the fingers, they were soft and gentle, like a doctor's.

'There was a whole crowd of them.'

'But what did they do?'

'One of them started touching me.'

A very tall boy had pulled a puce silk handkerchief from his breast pocket and had thrown it to Lingfield. All the time the tall boy had grinned from ear to ear. Not many years afterwards Gwynn had read in a newspaper that he had been tried and executed by the IRA for belonging to the SAS. He had wondered then if he still had the handkerchief.

'But, darling, you couldn't have come unless you wanted to. Did you?'

He could still see Lingfield's face looming over him, no expression of pleasure, present or future, but one of bored determination and disdain.

'Go on, did you?'

Immediately afterwards and ever since it had worried him. He had never been able to explain or understand his complaisance. In dreams, and even half awake, he had relished his recurrent victimization.

'Crécy, it was a long time ago, I can't remember.'

'It's so gross. What a turn-on!'

She pulled her lace skirt up and scratched her knee.

'And to think it was my father. Maybe we could blackmail him?'

Fat blobs of rain smacked against the smeary windows. The sexual correlation between abusing father and abused daughter stirred something in him. He knew that Lingfield was not a cornucopia, but that didn't mean he was a pauper. He mightn't provide a Tuscan farmhouse, but perhaps a trickle to help sustain an artist and his girl.

'What about your father?'

'What about him?'

Gwynn found that he was supplicatingly kneeling at Crécy's feet, his head resting against her thigh.

'Has he any money?'

'Oh, forget it. I was only joking.'

'I mean, couldn't he help a bit? He must be devoted to you.'

As an encouragement he stroked the soft skin of her inner thigh. A Fenland farmer friend had once described his soil as having the same silky consistency. He had never married.

'Are you crazy? Anyway, he's up to his eyeballs in hock.'

'Surely he'll leave you something?'

He rubbed her big toe.

'Not a hope. He's like Dostoevsky – determined to be doomed.'

Surprised, he lifted his head. That she had heard of Dostoevsky was unexpected, that she should liken her father to him was beyond comprehension.

'Are we talking about the same person?'

'Oh, he's probably changed since you knew him. What was he like?'

'Fun-loving philanderer, dashing dilettante, gambling and shooting, all the things the gossip columnists say about him.'

'Well, you know what they're like.'

'I didn't tell you, I saw him the other night?'

'Where?'

'At that Lebanese do in Eaton Square.'

'Why didn't you tell me?'

'He was spewing up blood. I didn't want to worry you.'

It was only half true. He had been frightened that she might have left him to cherish her father. And, though he couldn't exactly say why, he wasn't terribly keen for her father to know with whom she was living. Crécy eased away from him and giggled nervously.

'Crumbs! Last time I saw him he'd fainted and was lying on the floor.'

'I told him he ought to see a doctor.'

'That was kind.'

They sat in silence, Crécy picking at the chipped polish on her fingernails, Gwynn scrupulously rolling a cigarette.

He ambled to the gas jet. He wanted to sound nonchalant, but couldn't eliminate all trace of sulkiness from his voice.

'Oh well, bang goes all hope of Tuscany then.'

Crécy overlooked his remark. She lay musing on the sofa, an adult and calculating Alice.

'I've just had a thought.'

She hesitated. Gwynn murmured encouragement.

'There's a man called Travers ... '

Gwynn whipped away from her, but not in time; she'd glimpsed his confusion.

'Do you know him? He's sort of an art dealer. I thought ...'

'What's he said to you?'

Gwynn spoke to the wall. He sounded tense, straining to rein his fury. She wasn't sure whether she knew him well enough not to be scared.

'Nothing. I've never even met him. It's just that he's a friend of my brother, Briar, and I thought ... '

He swung round, all smiles and jollity.

'No more thoughts, darling; I tell you what, I'll take you out to dinner tonight.'

He kissed her on top of her head, then on her nose and then on her mouth. It was the first time he'd offered to take her out to dinner; it was the first time he'd called her darling. It was all rather confusing.

Chapter Eleven

IN a brand-new branch of fashionable J. C. Sweats
Croissant Kitchens sat a young couple clearly intriguing.
Croissants were all the rage. The *jeunesse dorée* could and
did eat them from sunrise till sunrise. They ate them
blueberry-flavoured, cinnamon-flavoured, stuffed with tuna
fish and even plain. The croissants in front of Crécy and Briar
were listed on the menu as 'Mudly Croissant'. They were
spattered with dark chocolate fudge.

The siblings, bitter adversaries from nursery days, viewed
each other over the table with the manifest mistrust that only
those most intimately bound can share. Their conversation was
all but drowned by a monotonous booming of African drums, a
feature of J. C. Sweats Kitchens.

'Crécy, I haven't much time, I've an important meeting with
Father Urban, so whatever – '

'You know your friend Travers?'

'What about him?'

Briar spoke peevishly and blushed. The effect in such a
winsome young face would have struck anyone but his sister as
charming. But she hardly noticed, she was trying to understand
why the mere mention of Travers should provoke annoyance.
Gwynn had instantly boiled over and now Briar had snapped at
her. Perhaps they were all part of a homosexual conspiracy.
She was beginning to have her doubts about the whole of the
opposite sex. And who was Father Urban?

'I just thought Travers was a friend of yours.'

'So? You surely haven't dragged me here to talk about my
friends.'

'I wonder whether he could help Gwynn.'

'And who be Gwynn?'

An inquisitive stranger might have had difficulty in determining their relationship. There was a family resemblance in their long, Plantagenet faces and their dark blue eyes, but their style of dress was perplexingly disparate and suggested very different backgrounds. Briar, in a tight-fitting grey silk tracksuit, neither stretched nor marked by bouts of vigorous exercise, was an exotic cat, probably Persian. His sister, in paint-spattered lumberjack's shirt and potato-sacking skirt was clearly an alley cat.

'You know, the man I live with.'

She regretted the expression the moment she uttered it. It was prim and proprietorial and showy-off. It reminded her with disgust of girls who waved around their newly acquired engagement rings with *soi-disant* insouciance. She bit savagely into her croissant and unwittingly garnished the tip of her nose.

'I never knew he had a name. Mother usually refers to him as your succour. But then she always was a rude bitch. What does he do when he's not succouring you?'

'He's a fantastic painter.'

'Of course.'

Briar dipped his little finger into the chocolate fudge and licked it with a shiver of disgust.

'How foul, they've put flour in it.'

For years they'd traded with each other in blows, insults, accusations and threats. Crécy knew that now in her altered circumstances none of these would be of the slightest avail. The only way was to plead with him. It was hard for her and very distasteful.

'You know my allowance has been stopped?'

'Frankly, I can only say I thought it was about time.'

Briar saw no point in adding that he had tried and failed to persuade his mother to augment his own allowance with his sister's.

'We're finding it terribly difficult to survive. You know what an artist's life is like.'

She knew perfectly well that he hadn't the faintest idea of what an artist's life was like. She was grovelling shamelessly and from his disdain she could see that she was succeeding.

'It's asking an awful lot, I know, but you see Gwynn *is* good and he's also extremely versatile ... '

Briar pushed his finger-pricked croissant aside and looked bored, as if his life was constantly subject to such blandishments.

'... and I just wondered whether you could possibly ask Travers to help.'

Briar lit a cigarette. There was a complacent emptiness about his expression, a look that Crécy took to mean she'd won.

'I'll have to think about it, old girl. It's true I have put the odd bit of business Travers' way, but it's all been important stuff.'

Crécy noted the use of 'old girl' with satisfaction. It was the warmest endearment he ever vouchsafed and was rarely employed.

'The thing is Gwynn's terribly adaptable.'

'What do you mean?'

'He can draw and paint in so many different styles.'

Briar was puzzled; he stopped trying to blow smoke rings. He looked at Crécy invitingly but she offered no elaboration. Then, very slowly, the light of comprehension flickered in his face. He leant across the table towards her and whispered.

'Do you mean that ... '

'If someone wants a Matisse, Gwynn can supply it. Yes, I do. And a Turner. And a Picasso. And ... '

Righteous indignation swept Briar's face. With a savage stab he sank his half-consumed cigarette into his croissant.

'That's the most disgraceful proposition. That somebody from this family ... '

But for all its fire and fury Briar's display of outrage somehow lacked conviction.

Chapter Twelve

BLISS woke dreading that the pain in his back might have gone. He sat up, breathed in and was relieved to find that it was still there. Throughout his life he had suffered from what he termed the Law of Ultimate Dereliction, LUD: a lesson learnt for school; a toothache for the dentist; an explanation for a slighted lover; all had evaporated at the critical moment. That morning he was due at the Brompton Hospital and to have arrived there symptomless would have been galling.

He rolled out of bed cheerfully. Somebody would diagnose the pain and then it could be eliminated. Brushing his teeth reminded him of a vivid dream he'd had in the night. He had been taking tea with the Queen and her husband and eldest son when, without warning, his teeth had crumbled from his gums. Knowing that if he could keep them in his mouth a dentist would be able to reinsert them, he had rushed from the Palace without so much as an adieu and wandered the streets searching for a dentist. But, not daring to open his mouth for fear of the teeth tumbling out, he had been unable to ask for directions.

He smiled into the mirror at his own credulity, then gently felt each tooth to be absolutely sure. In the dream it had all seemed real enough. He had even woken, from a dream in the dream, to find two rootless, rotten teeth hiding in his bedclothes.

At breakfast he made out his daily list. A girl called Bobo once suggested, neither without malice nor some truth, that it was his equivalent of morning prayer.

Ring Simon

54

Milk
Bread
Brompton Hospital
Paracetamol
Bobo Dinner?

Bobo was always good for a last-minute invitation. He felt remarkably well, hadn't felt so full of beans for ages. His breakfast was a delight, as if he'd never properly tasted food before: the buttered toast and marmalade a revelation of creamy bitter-sweetness, the coffee a perfect foil to it. He only regretted that he had not made himself bacon and eggs. Even the prospect of a telephone conversation with Simon could not dull his spirits or his appetite. He added to his list.

Arrange Cocktail Party
Make Date
    " guest list (30/40)
Discuss with Venetia

Why not? It was time he pulled himself out of the rut. He congratulated himself for remembering that Venetia had started her own catering company. Thirty to forty was probably on the low side; after all, not everyone would accept. He changed the numbers to fifty and sixty. He was quite excited, deciding on whom to invite was a pleasure he would delay until the evening when he and Bobo could make a list.

He glanced at the financial headlines in the paper. 'Market Steadies.' 'Toy Factory Closes.' 'Brewers' Dividend Held.' Then he turned to the front page. 'Damascus Devastated. Huge Loss of Life.' He was speculating on how that news would affect his Anglo-Syrians when he remembered with relief that he'd sold his holding six months ago.

'Simon, morning!'

'Hello, Bliss, you sound full of the joys.'

Bliss took a cigarette from a porcelain box and lit it as an accompaniment to his third cup of coffee. He hardly ever smoked.

'Doubtless you'll do your best to depress me.'

'Don't be like that. We only aim to please.'

'That's what worries me. I gather the market's steadied.'

'Only the gilts really. I don't think it's bottomed out yet.'

'Have you sold for me yet?'

'No, I'm ... '

'But Simon, we've only got a few days to go.'

'Honestly, Bliss, you must trust me. I believe that once it's reached bottom there'll be a marked upward turn.'

The coffee was tepid. Bliss lived in fear of finding a drowned fly in his cup. He stubbed out the half-finished cigarette in the saucer. He couldn't imagine how anyone could actually enjoy smoking.

'But Simon, when ... '

'And don't forget that with a depressed market there'll be a lot of bullish new time buyers at the end of the account.'

Bliss groaned inwardly. In Simon's hands he had all the resolution of a jellyfish.

'You've decided what to sell?'

'Of course, Bliss, I will only do the very best for you. By the way, didn't see you at the Carrs' thrash last night.'

'I decided to chuck at the last minute.'

'Your ex was there and Bobo Cooper with that shit, Manning-Pratley. Several people wondered what you were up to. Lavinia said you were in hospital. Must go, the other line's flashing.'

Bliss stood up and stretched. The trouble with feeling wonderful first thing in the morning was that one felt bloody ghastly later on. He wasn't particularly bothered that the Carrs hadn't invited him; he wouldn't have gone anyway. He crossed 'Bobo Dinner?' off his list. She was a predatory little tramp at the best of times.

Bliss had passed the hospital countless times but had never looked at it. Set back from the road behind high iron railings and dense shrubbery, it had the appearance of a seedy, second-class public school. The Victorian architect had aspired to instant venerability by straight recourse to Tudor gothic. Oriels and ivy clung to the diapered walls; there were crenellated towers and the windows were mullioned and latticed. Bliss arched his shoulders to ward off a descending cloud of gloom; doubtless leeches and tutsan were still in use.

He pushed open the studded door with rather less assurance than a new boy entering school for the first time.

The room he was shown into was trapezoid in shape. At one end of it stood a plain wooden desk. Scattered about were upright chairs. The walls were stark – no exhorting posters, only dead white paint. The longest wall for all its length and half its height was of mottled glass, which gave Bliss an eerie sensation of being submerged. He sat on a hard chair and waited. The room could have been empty for years.

Normally he loathed hospitals – delayed visiting ill friends and relatives until the last moment, when they were either cured or past consciousness at the point of death. At the age of ten he had been rushed to hospital in the middle of the night. There had been no room for him in the children's ward, so he had been put in a men's ward. The man in the bed next to his had gargled all night and smelled of excrement. The next morning the old boy was still and silent, and both of them had been moved. He did not mind this hospital, in spite of its ugliness and the characteristic smell of phenol. He liked the silence and absence of bustle. He liked the emptiness of the room. Perhaps it was only the room he was in that he liked.

He could still savour his prep school: chalk and cheap floor polish and in the winter terms mud and damp flannel. In the summer there had been the not unpleasant smells of boys' sweat and blanco and linseed oil. All this *à la recherche*, surely a sign of premature senility. Still no one came. Occasionally a wavering, refracted figure would soundlessly pass across the windows. He felt bereft of will, so that if nobody came to him he would remain patiently where he was till doomsday; hollow-headed and with a nervous teeming in his stomach. It was the same sensation that he had shamefully endured when he was four or five. He had called it feeling girlish, but had never spoken of it to anyone. Then the enfeeblement had been detestable; now he accepted it with equanimity. One of his earliest memories was of a small overflow pipe on the front of the house that reminded him of a tummy-button – there was a desirability ...

The door flew open with such force and lack of warning that Bliss instinctively leapt to his feet like a well-trained child.

'Late! Late! I'll be late for Judgment Day!'

57

A plump man bolted from the door towards the empty desk. 'I am Israel, Dr Israel. And you ... '

He grabbed the chair as if it might save him from drowning. Then, safely at his desk, he fumbled papers.

' ... you are Lord Leconfield. No, I tell a lie, Lord Lingfield.'

Dr Israel's principal distinguishing mark was his bushy black moustache. In his passage across the room there had been suggestions of both Groucho Marx and the White Rabbit. Both were too pronounced to be unintentional. Bliss detested self-disparagement; when practised by professionals it was unforgivable.

'So, you have a pain in the back? That's better than being one in the neck.'

The doctor laughed alone. Bliss wondered what it was like being Jewish, if one felt different. The only Jew he knew was Simon and he used to go to chapel at school.

'To find out what is causing the pain we have to make a diagnosis.'

He still had a book at home that had belonged to his father as a child. It was called *Round the Wonderful World*. In it the Jews of Jerusalem were described as being ' ... the least attractive of all. They seem afraid of being hit.' It was the only passage from the book that had stuck in his mind.

'First, I want you to cough. No, harder. Bring up some phlegm. Good, now spit in the bowl.'

Bliss put his hand to his moustache and ran his fingers over it. The doctor smiled at him.

'It's all right, it's perfectly clean. As you can see, I have the same problem, it's the only drawback to a moustache. I like soft-boiled eggs, but I only dare eat them in the privacy of my home.'

The doctor had dark, humorous eyes. Bliss couldn't be sure whether it was a mocking humour or an amiable one. He had heard that Jews considered themselves the world's élite.

'In a few minutes we are going to take some X-rays of your chest. After that I want to have a look round your lungs, maybe take a sample or two. I have to put a bronchoscope, sort of tube, down. It's a little uncomfortable, so you'll be sedated. Now, do you have any questions?'

Dr Israel folded his hands together and rested his arms on

the desk. Beaming, he looked like a lecturer who had just dazzled an eminent audience. Bliss struggled to think of a question, he was sure it would be very bad-mannered not to ask one.

'Are you an orthodox Jew?'

Dr Israel might have been asked such a question twice a day by every one of his patients, he showed neither surprise nor impatience.

'As a matter of fact, I am.'

'Were you born over here?'

'No, in Germany. In Heilsbronn.'

'And during the war ... any trouble?'

Bliss questioned the doctor with the tenacity and apathy of a guest burdened with a bore at a cocktail party.

'Trouble?'

'Concentration camp. That sort of thing.'

'For me, no. I was fortunate. My family was not so lucky.'

'I'm sorry.'

The tone of the last remark was without a trace of sympathy. Bliss might have been apologizing for bumping into somebody on the Underground.

'Lord Lingfield, I really meant whether there was anything you wanted to ask me about yourself.'

'Me! No, I just can't think why you're making all this song and dance about a pain in the back.'

'Shall we go down to the X-ray then?'

They stood up. The doctor was a foot shorter than his patient and running to fat. But, even beyond their moustaches and grey pinstripe suits, there was a resemblance.

'Lord Lingfield, it's important for a patient to trust his doctor.'

'I hardly know you.'

In the passage two nurses passed the black-haired men.

'Has Dr Israel got a brother?'

'How should I know?'

'Was that his son with him then?'

'His son's dead, silly.'

At the top of a flight of stairs Dr Israel paused and turned to Bliss.

'You do know what sort of specialist I am?'
'No idea.'
'Ah, I thought as much.'
And then they descended.

Chapter Thirteen

A wheezy Lady Lingfield pushed open her door and trundled in her wheeled wickerwork shopping-basket. She had dressed too warmly for the day and, glowing and parched, fell on the sofa exhausted by her morning's expedition. Because of her brother's prodigality all shopping on account had had to be abandoned and goods could no longer be ordered by telephone. There was an ominous silence from Clarry's room, she wondered whether he had had the temerity to disobey her express command only to go out with her permission. It was nearly lunchtime, she would have a smidgen of gin and a lot of tonic and then try to get Bliss on the telephone again. Before her shopping spree she had spent a good twenty minutes ringing his number without success. It was extremely inconsiderate of him, actually bad-mannered, to be out when his own mother wanted to talk to him, especially as he was her only child.

Altogether it had been a frustrating morning; Harrods no longer stocked 'Mr Eveready's Master Touch Meals' and the health food shop had sold out of the magazine *Fruit and Fibre*. Worse, a man she had been to see about Clarry's future had been most discouraging.

'And your brother, Lady Lingfield, does not require constant medical attention?'

'Good heavens no! He's as fit as a fiddle.'

'And continent?'

Lady Lingfield had blushed as instinctively as a schoolgirl and nodded her head enthusiastically.

'Now we come to his mental state. How would you describe him? Eccentric, odd, feeble-minded, mad, sane?'

'Oh, dear Clarry is completely normal.'

'No quirks?'

'Quite quirkless.'

The interviewer had put down his pen, folded his hands as if in prayer and only after an age spoken.

'I'm sorry, Lady Lingfield, but try as I might, I can think of no good reason for your brother to go into an old people's home.'

In desperation Lady Lingfield had wondered whether to mention Clarry's counting mania but realized that it was too late to backtrack. Dispirited and void of ideas she had left.

She sat with the telephone receiver at her ear stupefied by the unanswered ringing tone and by a large housefly that appeared to be studying her from an ashtray. It tipped forwards on its front legs and used its back legs to clean its wings. Then it rubbed its back legs together like a fastidious person drying his hands. All the while it seemed to be examining her. She was too numbed to think of swatting it. And then it occurred to her that the black, bulbous eyes watching her were Bliss's. Her grandfather who had served in India had scared her as a child with tales of such magic. He had called it the science of transmog – something. It would be so like her son to turn himself into a prying, loathsome insect when she most needed his help. She shook her head like someone coming out of a dream and replaced the receiver. The fly moved confidently around the rim of the ashtray; she was tempted now to strike it but the legacy of her childhood held her back.

It was definitely gin time. There was still no sound from Clarry's room, but to be on the safe side she sidled the gin and tonic into her glass and decided she could abstain from noisy ice. Then taking up pad and pencil she settled herself comfortably into an armchair. She put her glass on the table beside her – it would be a reward. At the top of the pad she wrote, 'Remember to tell Bliss' and underlined it twice. She sucked the pencil ruminatively, couldn't remember whether doing so would give her lead poisoning and then continued.

1 Clarry steals and sells (for petty sums) the family heirlooms.
2 Embarrassing exhibitionism in Calcutta Court.
3 Malicious sneering at me – his own little sister.
4 Counting mania.

5 V. nasty personal habits which I have to clear up.
6 Disobedience.
7 Deliberately talks gibberish and is proud of it.
8 Makes exasperating, grunting noises in my company.

She sucked the pencil again and, deciding that she had written a sufficiently full and true indictment to convict Clarry in her son's eyes, she put aside the pad and stretched out for her rewarding glass of gin. As she raised it to her lips and before she was able to take a sip Clarry's leery face peeked at her from round his door.

'Three hundred thousand, I've just reached three hundred thousand. Oh! Naughty, naughty! Drinking gin all by yourself again.'

Chapter Fourteen

'THERE'S no point in beating about the bush.'

Dr Israel clutched a bundle of envelopes. The room was not the austere one in which Bliss and he had earlier met. In the fireplace stood a bowl of dried flowers and on the walls there were bright, exuberant water-colours of roses. High up, the room looked out over trees. The doctor too was different: composed, less determinedly jocose. Bliss wondered if there was some crafty psychological reason for the changes.

'I take it you would like me to speak to you man to man?'

Bliss couldn't imagine how else they could converse and smiled affirmation. On the mantelshelf were displayed framed family photographs and, perplexingly, a row of some half dozen ordinary-looking pebbles.

'Presumably you have an idea as to why you're here?'

Bliss nodded enthusiastically. The pebbles reminded him of his earliest memory. His nanny had given him a shiny red tin bucket decorated with pictures of Mickey Mouse. For a whole summer he had used it to collect gravel from the driveway of Lingfield Place. He couldn't remember what he had done with the gravel, but he knew that the pastime had given him an intense, almost mystical pleasure.

'I have to tell you that the diagnosis was not good.'

Dr Israel looked solemn, a judge about to pronounce sentence. Bliss was put in mind of a blurred photograph of Mr Justice Darling wearing the black cap, there was a resemblance.

Outside high banks of gilded white clouds moved south. Bliss prided himself on his sense of direction; it was a legacy from his army days.

'At the same time I don't want you to take an unduly gloomy or alarmist attitude.'

In a way, he wished he hadn't thought of the Mickey Mouse bucket because it reminded him of Nanny and he felt guilty about her. It was she who had first called him Bliss. 'Master Bliss, when you grow up anything you want in the world can be yours.' Every birthday, every Christmas she sent him a card and a pound note. He hadn't seen her for twenty years or more. She was in a home for geriatrics now. He hated feeling guilty, perhaps when he was better he would find time to visit her.

'There are plenty of people walking the streets of London who have, to a varying degree, mastered cancer.'

Bliss tried to catch the doctor's eye but he had his eyes down. He might have been assessing a particularly tricky bridge hand.

'I hadn't realized. That had never occurred to me ... whereabouts?'

'The lung.'

Bliss smiled under his moustache. He thought of Cleanands Mines and Simon and Moyra and how they could all go to hell.

'How long have I got?'

'Oh, you're not terminal.'

He was not one of the great London termini, he was just a tuppenny country halt. His smile crept from under his moustache.

'What are my chances?'

'I'm sorry, I'm not a gambling man. I can only tell you that you are one of the quarter of the population who develops cancer. Did either of your parents contract it?'

Bliss felt delightfully light-hearted, a host of threats expunged.

'My father was killed in a road accident, and my mother is still alive.'

'I'm sorry – about your father, I mean. Tell me, have you been subject to unusual distress recently?'

Bliss was engrossed. He was adding to his list of people and things that could now go to hell. There were his vulturine children; his mother; money; the necessity to sell his house; prodigal Clarry; Bobo; money; Lavinia; money and the take-over of his country by reds, blacks and Jews. He was confident that with very little effort he would be able to think of many more.

'Lord Lingfield, you're not with me. Have you been under stress lately?'

Dr Israel was an exponent of the school that held that stress was a primary carcinogen. He had written several monographs on the subject. He peered at his patient. He seemed curiously unmoved, or rather, with his air of abstracted nonchalance, he appeared to be mildly amused.

'No more than usual.'

Bliss smiled. It was a weary, slightly dismissive smile. Dr Israel half expected it to be accompanied by a languid, scornful gesture of the hand.

'I'm bound to say, Lord Lingfield, your attitude is extraordinarily phlegmatic.'

'These things happen.'

'You put me out of countenance.'

Dr Israel got up and stood by the mantelpiece. He lightly fingered the pebbles on the shelf. The two men smiled at each other.

'Some of my patients wish to know as little as possible about their treatment, merely when and where they should show up. Others like to know exactly what is going on. How about you?'

'I'd like to hear all about it.'

He sounded as if he were making a polite enquiry about an acquaintance's holiday. Dr Israel shuddered and returned to the refuge of his desk. He tried not to look at Lord Lingfield – whenever he did his eye was caught by an apparently mocking gaze. He spoke rapidly, he wanted the consultation to be over.

'There are five cancer treatments: surgery, radiation, hormone therapy, chemotherapy and immunotherapy. Unfortunately, only about fifteen per cent of lung cancers are operable and yours is not one of them. Immunotherapy ... '

Bliss had always enjoyed being talked about, not behind his back but either directly or obliquely. He could still remember the words his nanny had used when discussing him with a rival nanny, ' ... always washes his hands the minute they get dirty and when he's finished playing in the sandpit he brushes the sand from his legs.'

66

'... perhaps one in a hundred thousand inoperable cancers will spontaneously regress. Call it a miracle, call it an answer to prayer. Call it what you like.'

Bliss plumped for miracle though he'd never thought much about thaumaturgy.

'Certain foods are beneficial. Eggs, liver, garlic, honey, yoghurt, kelp ... '

'So that's why we fought for the Falklands.'

He alone was amused by his joke. He envied those who'd seen action in the South Atlantic. His years of soldiering had been prosaically peaceful. Once during manoeuvres in Germany a fellow officer had lost an ear in a tank accident. A replacement had been found for him in the local mortuary, but it was a grotesque match: the wrong shape, the wrong size, even the wrong colour.

'... it is significantly interesting that descendants of subjects who have been afflicted with certain types of cancer are exposed to a higher risk than the rest of the population. For instance smokers who have had a parent with lung cancer are fourteen times more likely to develop lung cancer themselves than smokers whose parents did not have the disease.'

It irked Bliss that he could not remember the officer's name, particularly as he had bumped into him in the Duke of Wellington pub not so long ago. He had wanted then to ask him if the alien ear had been a handicap as far as women were concerned but decided that they were not sufficiently well acquainted.

'... unpleasant side-effects, such as sickness and hair loss. And, through lowering immunity, chemotherapy can facilitate the growth of the tumour and lead to microbial, viral and fungal infections.'

Bliss's smile stretched across his face. He tried to curb it, he didn't want the good doctor who was taking so much trouble to think he was flippant or inattentive. But he had had a stupendous idea. He would write a final list, a sort of epilogue, the list of lists. On one side he would record all those people and things which had given him happiness in his life and on the other all those that had displeased him. Thus would he pronounce his last judgment on the temporal world.

'So we come down to radiotherapy. As a palliative it is

irreplaceable for localized but inoperable tumours such as yours. You'll be an in-patient at the Marsden Hospital over the road. The thrice-weekly treatment is for three weeks. It is not particularly pleasant, some of my patients complain of tiredness, nausea, burns.'

Bliss was searching for headings for his two categories. Pro and Con would do, but were commonplace, as indeed were Good and Bad. He liked U and Non-U, but didn't want it to be thought that he was snobbish.

'From time to time misleading, and in my view reprehensible statistics are published. For instance, there is a widespread belief that a five-year remission virtually amounts to a cure. Unfortunately, the reason the number of recurrences drops off after five years is principally because the number of survivors has also drastically dropped by then.'

Saints and Sinners, Gentlemen and Players, Grace and Disfavour, Wheat and Chaff. None of them was adequate.

'I want you to know that I am always available. Here are my phone numbers. If ever you feel worried or distressed ring me here or at my home, I won't mind.'

Bliss took the card and scarcely glanced at it. He had, after all, found his headings. He knew his jubilation was childish, he didn't mind. Pleasures and Regrets. He rolled the words around his mouth, they dripped like honey from his tongue. He knew that they were right, that they could not be bettered. They smacked of fastidiousness, they rang with literary elegance, their sang-froid was patrician. He was impatient to be home so that he could inscribe them.

'Is there anything you want to ask me?'

Bliss stirred in his chair and chuckled.

'What's the history of the pebbles on the mantelshelf?'

'My eight-year-old son collected them on holiday in Cornwall.'

'Rum sort of thing to keep.'

'Sentimental, I agree. But it was his last holiday, he died of leukaemia soon afterwards.'

Outside the sun shone in the matt blue sky.

Chapter Fifteen

I T SAT upon the crest of the rise, an elephantine, grey concrete molar bristling with metal protuberances. Mother Euberta and Bel saw it unexpectedly as their small car rounded the bend.

'God in heaven! What on earth is that?'

Nowadays Bel rarely sallied forth either in London or the country. Change and innovation shocked and grieved her, which was why she preferred to stay at home. It was a sad irony that because she went out so rarely there was always sure to be some new degradation to pain her when she did.

'Is it something nuclear?'

Even Francis who was propped up on a tattered cushion on the back seat appeared to be interested. He forsook his ball of crumpled paper and beadily eyed the monolith.

'Oh, nothing like that.'

Reverend Mother knew exactly what it was; her father had been a civil engineer. She regretted that she had not taken another road, but she had forgotten Bel's aversion to the march of progress.

'It's a pile for the overhead section of the projected motorway.'

It loomed over the gently sloping hill that ran down to the meandering river and valley below.

'A motorway in the Shoreham valley! It's unthinkable. Nobody could be so barbaric.'

'The locals are mostly for it. It'll take the heavy traffic away from their narrow village streets.'

'What would the Ancients have made of it, Euberta?'

'I've seen the plans, it could be worse. I thought we'd have our picnic on that hill above Dunstall Priory.'

69

'You know Palmer particularly liked the sixty-fifth psalm. You remember the line, "And the little hills shall rejoice on every side." It's nothing less than sacrilege, whatever you may say to defend it.'

'Well, it'll soon be out of sight.'

'Not seeing it doesn't mean it isn't still there.'

'Lunch will restore you.'

'That "thing" has quite spoilt my appetite.'

They motored on in silence and Francis returned to his paper ball.

Bel had fled to Lingfield Place as soon as she had heard her nephew's casually imparted, horrifying news. On the train down she had galvanized and then embarrassed her fellow passengers by beseeching them to pray for Bliss to be healed. 'Sometimes a battery of prayer forces God to listen.' In the three days that she had been at the convent she had uncustomarily attended all the divine offices and piqued some of the nuns with her scrupulous devotion. She had risen early, eaten frugally, and even been seen pottering about the kitchen-garden. It was sarcastically said that it was the first time she had been on retreat and not on holiday. Francis seemed to be similarly afflicted. Usually when he was at the convent he became over-excited and behaved like a delinquent, but this time he had stolen nothing and hardly hollered or hooted. With all this sanctimoniousness about, Reverend Mother had feared that a pernicious depression might sweep through the community. To nip it in the bud she had proposed the picnic trip to Shoreham in the hope that it would humour Bel and, for that matter, Francis too. Few influences were more conducive to melancholy in a holy order than a cheerless capuchin.

Reverend Mother had chosen Shoreham for a number of shrewd reasons. Because of Bel's mystic affection for the secluded, rather jumbled town and its one-time denizens – Palmer, Calvert and Richmond – it had become a tradition that whenever she stayed at the convent at least one pilgrimage should be made to Shoreham. Bel herself had said that while she was there she invariably forgot about herself and her worries and revelled instead in the history and beauty of the

70

place. A less elevated reason and one that Reverend Mother would never have admitted to anyone, indeed barely allowed herself to contemplate, was the fate of Bel's collection of paintings. It was common knowledge that she had not finally settled on a beneficiary. It was less commonly acknowledged that next to God the Order loved endowments.

They sat upon a grassy knoll. Behind them straggled a copse of spindly trees. Below them the ground dipped softly down to a valley that ran away into a hill-enfolded dell. Francis nibbled an apple and fingered the fringes of a plaid travelling rug.

'To think we're less than twenty miles from Westminster.'

There was not a building in sight. Only the occasional sound of a darting bird broke the silence. It was the sort of silence that hummed. In the distance a herd of black and white cows moved listlessly, almost imperceptibly. There wasn't a single human being in view to disfigure the scene.

'Palmer would have appreciated this. To think of that poor, dear man ending his days in a hideous villa in Redhill.'

Reverend Mother brushed crumbs from her lap and took another sandwich. By some standards their picnic would have been considered sparse and dull; by theirs it was Lucullan. It was spread out on a white tea-towel: two hard-boiled eggs, some Marmite sandwiches, two green apples. A thermos contained tea.

'Tuck in, Bel dear, or I'll scoff the lot.'

Staring ahead, Bel absent-mindedly peeled an egg and shook salt from a small twist of wax-paper.

'I sometimes wonder if I'm the only member of my family to be aware of beauty. Perhaps Bliss, now that his life is in the balance, will turn to it for comfort. But he's reacted so strangely. I well remember a Japanese film, what was it called ... ?'

'It seems to me as if your nephew is behaving in an admirably Christian fashion, embracing death and salvation.'

'But he doesn't believe in salvation, he has no faith at all. He just hates life.'

'Does Francis like Marmite?'

'Not much.'

'He can have my egg. I don't think we can pretend to

71

understand other people's attitudes and ambitions any more than they can be expected to explain them.'

'You can't really call death an ambition.'

'Oh, certainly.'

Reverend Mother stood up and stretched; she was a strong, healthy woman. In her youth she had played county championship tennis. She sat down again and began peeling the egg for Francis, catching the bits of shell in the voluminous folds of her black habit.

'Well, I still think his life can be saved if enough people pray passionately.'

'H'm ... '

Reverend Mother quartered the egg and handed a piece to Francis who took it with consummate daintiness. He removed the yolk from the white and rolled it into a ball before popping it into his mouth.

'You're possibly right, but it's a paradox, isn't it?'

Bel masticated methodically. Years ago a fellow rambler had told her that he had never needed to see a doctor because he chewed every mouthful of food at least twenty times. It was a while before she could speak.

'What's a paradox?'

'Praying for Bliss to live when he wants to die.'

Bel took a bite of a Marmite sandwich. Eating gave her time to think.

'But, Euberta, you wouldn't hesitate to prevent someone committing suicide.'

Reverend Mother's expression was fey, her eyes cast on some complex truth beyond any human horizon. It was a countenance mistrusted and detested by her inferiors, especially the novices.

'It's strange how often goodness requires evil to precipitate it.'

'Now that surely can't be right.'

Men in yellow gumboots and motley wind-cheaters carrying sticks and poles appeared on the hillside opposite.

'Without the evil of betrayal there would have been no Crucifixion.'

'Now that's a red herring and you know it, Euberta.'

'Of course, as Simone Weil said, "Evil is to love, what

72

mystery is to the intelligence." You know I knew her?'

'You couldn't have done.'

'It was when she was at the Grosvenor Sanatorium at Ashford, not far from here. I was a probationer nurse there.'

'You never told me before. What was she like?'

'Stubborn and composed. She took no food, occasionally allowed one of us to wet her lips with sherry.'

The yellow-booted men split into small groups and moved apart.

'You know, Bel, it is very silly of us to think we can understand anything. Theology is after all only an exercise in logic, and whoever said that God was a logician?'

The groups of men on the hillside and those now in the valley formed a pattern.

'It's like prayer – why do we do it when we know that God is humanly incomprehensible? At best it's a form of self-examination; at worst it's a superstitious vanity. But to think that one can have dialogue with God – poof!'

'Really, Euberta, I hope you don't talk like this in the community, you sound like that wretched man at Cambridge.'

'Have no fear, I would still be a Christian even if I became convinced that there was no God and that we were merely accidents in chaos.'

'That doesn't help at all. I think we ought to be going, Francis is getting restless.'

The capuchin had wandered down the hillside and was watching the men intently.

Bel stood up. In spite of the rug, bits of greenery clung to her tweed skirt.

'What do you suppose those men down there are doing? Are they farm labourers?'

'They look more like surveyors to me. By the way, Bel, I was only teasing; of course we'll pray for Bliss like billy-ho.'

Other reactions to the news of Bliss's illness varied among his family, friends and acquaintances. They were not as universally sympathetic as a sick man might have hoped for or even expected. Bliss, though aware of a certain coolness, put it down to the traditional English distaste for disease, infirmity and disability.

Wandering aimlessly in Battersea Park's small municipal zoo, Briar and his friend Travers peered expectantly into cages.

'Sorry to hear about your father.'

'Oh, Dad!'

'Anything they can do?'

'Haven't a clue. All I know is that the old man's got Big C. Isn't that a jackal?'

'Says here it's a fennec.'

'Do you suppose there's any money to be made out of being a Lord – you know, endorsing socks and saying how jolly good MacBlah's whisky is?'

'You might get somebody mug enough to put you on the board of some dodgy company.'

'Do you remember telling me about some bod doing his mother in and never regretting it? Was that gospel?'

'Of course.'

'God, the female sex is disgusting. Just look at that.'

In a large, bare cage a red and purple rumped baboon looked at her mate with jaded desire. He, in a far corner, continued to manipulate his pink penis, his eyes revealing his resigned contempt for all about him. Arm in arm a flaunting youth and his petite, perky girl cast their eyes from the monkeys to the two fine young men, nudged each other and winked. Briar took Travers' elbow and withdrew him, he hated *hoi* giggly *polloi*.

'That reminds me, my sister's living with some painter bloke.'

'So?'

'They're pushed for money.'

'I never lend, darling.'

'According to my sister, he's a brilliant plagiarist.'

'You mean faker.'

'I only mentioned him because my sister begged me to.'

'You know I wouldn't be caught dead handling that sort of stuff. What's his name?'

'Gwynn.'

They paused to watch an old man with a stick trying to extract carrots and bits of apple from an empty stall.

'How old's this Gwynn fellow?'

'Forties, fifties, I'm just guessing, I've never met him.'

74

Travers wrinkled his nose like a hound scenting and then, grasping Briar by the shoulder, marched towards the zoo exit.

'You know you're a very brash boy, Briar. We'll go to my flat, there's something I want to talk to you about.'

The large and panelled dining-room at Terrick House was on the first floor; a preposterous arrangement, as the kitchens were in the basement. It contained two dining-tables. One, that dominated the centre of the room, could accommodate fifty people, but in these hard times was rarely required to seat more than twenty. And another, a pretty oval table set by the bay window overlooking the river, was used when the family ate alone. Teddy-Bear and Moyra sat there now. Not having much to say they watched the juggernauts hurtling along the Embankment and were in turn watched over by some dour family portraits. Moyra put down her fork; at her Paris finishing school, she had been taught that conversation was an art as indispensable to civilized living as gastronomy.

'Typical Bliss.'

Teddy-Bear succeeded in getting a forkful of lamb cutlet into his mouth as Moyra spoke and thus gained himself a few minutes' grace before he needed to reply. He detested pointless talk and considered that ninety-nine per cent of all talk was pointless. Besides, he had been interested in following the progress of a swaddled old woman on the pavement who was trying to pull one laden pram and at the same time push another. Furthermore, he didn't like thinking about Bliss, let alone discussing him.

'What?'

'The way he gets out of things.'

'What's he supposed to have done?'

'Oh God! Don't you ever listen to anything I say?'

Another thing about talk was how inflammable it was. There he had been quietly enjoying the prospect and his luncheon and then with two seemingly innocuous remarks he had set off a row.

'I'm sorry, my mind must have been elsewhere.'

'Your mind's only on your stomach.'

He longed to fight back, or at least show a semblance of resistance, but as always he could not think of a riposte either witty or retaliatory.

75

'I told you days ago that he'd got cancer.'

'Oh, poor chap, I am sorry.'

'Poor chap be damned! He's just doing what he's done all his life – copping out.'

Perhaps the worst thing about talk was how it filibustered eating. His favourite food in summer was cold lamb cutlets and in winter hot lamb cutlets and now that he had lamb cutlets in front of him he was prevented from enjoying them by the curse of conversation. Moyra was looking at him oddly, as if she supposed that he was gaga.

'I don't see how you can blame someone for being ill.'

'Knowing Bliss, he won't just leave it at that, he'll go the whole hog and snuff it.'

Women had always puzzled Teddy-Bear; Moyra baffled him. If she loathed her ex-husband as whole-heartedly as she claimed, surely the expectation of his imminent extinction was a cause for discreet rejoicing rather than renewed rancour. The only woman he had ever understood had been Nanny and he supposed she wasn't really a woman.

'Just when a father's influence is most needed, just when the children are at their most difficult and extravagant. He's always been useless but you would have thought that just once in his life he could ... '

Once again Moyra had spoilt his meal. He pushed a green bean around the rim of his plate.

'And I don't suppose he's got any money left to leave the children. Even if he has he'll leave it to one of those ghastly common sluts he beds.'

Teddy-Bear could eat no more. He put his knife and fork together and wondered whether Moyra would notice and complain about the food he had left. He wished that he was not such a temperate man, that he could summon anger at will.

'I wish you'd say something, can't you see how infuriating his behaviour is?'

It occurred to him how fortunate Bliss was to be leaving this vale of tears. He actually rather envied him. The thought tickled him. Moyra droned on.

'I wouldn't put it past Bliss to have engineered the whole ploy simply to exasperate me.'

Teddy-Bear felt a *frisson* between his stomach and his heart.

76

It was a new sensation, he wondered if it might be the prelude to anger. It swam to his head. He spoke and his voice shocked and thrilled him.

'That's enough, Moyra. What you say is as obnoxious as it is idiotic. Nobody but you could blame a man for dying.'

While Clarry, in an extraordinarily long pair of boxer trunks and in the privacy of his room, hummed and fashioned a crude whistle from a thick twig he had found in the park, his sister lay beached upon her bed. She had been asleep but had awakened in what she took to be the waste of night. The light beyond her partly-opened curtains was reddish-blue, the colour of uncooked meat; there wasn't a sound from the street below.

She knew now what had roused her. A gnawing pain like acute hunger but compounded with pangs of horrid fear gripped and held her. She was terribly awake.

There was a soft scratching, clicking sound. She couldn't tell from where it came – perhaps the inside of her head.

Hubert, her husband (how she missed him!) often used to say, 'I've experienced fear and the only thing to do is to confront it and analyze it.'

She kept a tin of biscuits on her bedside table but she knew that they could not conquer her swarming panic. It was partly to do with the disappearance of the two Chinese porcelain rabbits that had habitually stood on either side of the tallboy in the drawing-room. She had noted their absence that very morning and had immediately questioned Clarry. He, needless to say, had denied ever having seen them. She hadn't liked to ask the cleaning woman outright, they took offence so easily and were harder than ever to replace. Oddly enough, she had got Mrs Spurgeon through her haberdasher's brother-in-law. That was worry number one: either the rabbits were broken or they had been stolen.

Number two was the drinks. The contents of the assorted bottles in the drinks cupboard were waning at a prodigious rate. Somebody was nobbling them. She had surreptitiously sniffed Mrs Spurgeon's breath but detected nothing more incriminating than a nasty odour resembling minty Brussels sprouts. She suspected her brother, but it was hard to be sure because his erratic behaviour was always suggestive of inebriation. It wasn't the loss of the drink, though prices being what they were that was a consideration; it was the uneasiness of living in a home where there could be no trust.

And then there was Bliss. He lay behind all her anxieties, aggravating even those in which he hardly played a part. She knew a mother should not lean on her children but he was the only sane member of her family left. (She couldn't count the grandchildren; like all of their generation they were exclusively self-interested.) It was enough to make a mother weep: that at the hour of her greatest need her only child should be *hors de combat*.

She was mentally composing the fourth fear when she caught sight of a malevolent, weaselly face outside her window. She shut her eyes. She opened her eyes. It was still there. She tried to scream for Clarry, useless though she knew he would be, but no sound came save a faint, throaty rasp. She blinked – just to be sure. It was not a dream. The face belonged to a man and he was now visible from the waist up. In one hand he held a cloth with which he appeared to be attempting to break the glass. Or perhaps it was drenched with chloroform. Lady Lingfield ducked under the bedclothes. The dreadful gnawing had given way to a tremendous heart-pounding. That the man had paid her no heed made him and his purpose infinitely terrifying. It was hot and airless under the bedclothes, noisy too with the rapid thumping of her heart. She wondered how the man had been able to climb up on the outside to the third floor. And then she had a brilliant idea. Instead of submissively cowering in bed waiting for ravishment or worse she would leap up, rush across the room, burst open the window and pitch the miscreant to the street below.

She was halfway across the room when she recognized her wouldbe violator as the window-cleaner, a man frequently summoned but rarely seen. With a skittish wave and a gummy, ferocious smile she managed to turn on her heel and, still travelling briskly, made for the sanctuary of the bathroom.

The image in the mirror over the basin was blanched and crumple-faced, with tousled hair and nightdress disarrayed. Lady Lingfield had never felt so fatigued. She sat on the lavatory and wept sweet tears of self-pity.

Chapter Sixteen

HIS chest purple, marked like a woaded ancient Briton, Bliss lay on top of his bed in Swann Ward resting after his second treatment of radiation. On a bed-table lay a notebook in which he was listing his Pleasures and Regrets. Under Pleasures he had written, 'To lie under a scintillatingly leafy beech tree with a blue sky beyond, a Virginia cigarette at hand and a light-hearted cricket match in view.' It was a cheaty entry because it was not his own observation but his grandfather's. However, it sounded so idyllically English that he couldn't resist borrowing it. Underneath he had written 'Tilbury'.

Before being admitted he had dreaded the enforced intimacy of a public ward, but now that he had become established he was amused to find how much he relished the vagaries and peculiarities of his fellow patients. The diversity of their interests and attitudes was also a surprise. They all – well, not all, but some of them – had led far fuller lives and were more entertaining than any of his own friends. Surnames were unknown, intimacy was immediate and uncluttered with superfluous background or social assessment. Max had been in his time a nancy, soldier, artist's model, zoo attendant, croupier, novice monk and apparently whatever else entered his head. John, one of Bliss's neighbours, volunteered only that he was a thirty-year-old taxi driver from Ealing, but he made up for his reticence about himself with a rich repertoire of lewd limericks. He composed them, too, and had promised to dedicate one to Bliss. His other neighbour, Bill, was a broken-down rag-and-bone man. He alleged that he had once bought a sketch for five bob which he had sold to a dealer for twenty-five pounds, the dealer in turn had sold it at Christie's for two thousand, two hundred guineas. It was by Rembrandt and it had been reported in the press, he'd got the cuttings at home to prove it. So he said. George was a walking *Timeform* and would bribe the nurses with straight tips to lay his bets for him. The camaraderie was inspiring; Bliss had never felt such affinity with his fellows before, not at school, not in the army. It pleased him that his friends outside would probably accuse him of making a cult of the nobility of the common man. But they, leading their vapid, tinsel lives, wouldn't understand that death was the greatest uniter.

> Sceptre and crown
> Must tumble down
> And in the dust be equal made
> With the poor crooked scythe and spade.

The old boy who had written that certainly knew what he was talking about. Of all the inmates of Swann Ward only Frank, in the bed by the door, was silent and morose. But then it was generally and sometimes loudly agreed that he had no time left to make new friends.

Bliss closed his eyes. Only in hospital could one doze at any hour of the day without a feeling of guilt. No telephone. No daily bulletin of catastrophe from Simon. No merciless, unwanted chatter. Closed eyes were a sufficient indication to all but the nurses that the inmate did not wish to be disturbed. In the background he could hear John and George amiably disputing the pre-eminence of English food, or were they discussing the World Cup? Frank's breath rattled in his throat. Mentally Bliss touched wood, not one of the vaunted side-effects had afflicted him yet. The back-pain was still there but it was no worse. Bill swore that his treatment had made him lose his hair, but it seemed more likely that he had lost it naturally years ago. John had burns and George suffered from bouts of nausea. No doubt his own time would come. He wondered what day of the week it was and hoped it was not the weekend when visitors mostly came. Visitors were a nuisance, they upset the rhythm, just like exeats from school. So far, he had only had to endure his mother and Bobo. The former had exhausted him with her catalogue of misfortunes and the latter

80

had burst into tears on seeing him. Much to John's undisguised amusement she had been banished forthwith.

Bliss looked about him. He had no idea whether he had dozed for two minutes or two hours. On his bedside table lay the fruits of illness: a tub of potted shrimps, some tangerines, a sprig of fuchsia and half-a-dozen lamentably unfunny get-well cards. He picked up his notebook of Pleasures and Regrets. Why Tilbury?

He had been taken to Tilbury when he was four or five. He had gone with his parents to wave goodbye to an uncle who was sailing to Australia. 'Australia's a very long way away, it's the other side of the world.' So Tilbury was the threshold of the ends of the earth, a town hanging on the edge of nowhere. He dimly remembered it: vast and full of steam and smoke and incessant noisy movement, frightening and at the same time thrilling. He thought of it now as a place of finality, beyond which there was only a great gaping greyness that bleared into infinity. He knew he would return there. One day when he was better. There was something in Tilbury he had to discover.

John stretched an arm across the bed divide and prodded Bliss.

'Here you are. What do you think of it?'

Bliss took the sheet of paper, sat up a bit and read:

> A dapper young fella called Bliss,
> Tried to give our Ward Sister a kiss;
> She flung her legs wide
> And pulled him inside
> And now she's no longer a miss.

A thin-haired padre, young and brimful with *bonhomie* and evangelical aspirations appeared in the doorway. Instinctively Bliss closed his eyes. He wondered what it was that Tilbury would reveal. That indeed was a suitable subject for reflection.

Chapter Seventeen

I N A glumly anonymous area of north London, so drear that no district apparently claimed it, stood a shabby pub. The houses that had once provided its custom had long since gone, replaced now by billboards that fronted barren, waste-strewn patches. The pert gaudiness of the billboards was in grotesque contrast to the sombreness of the Edwardian pub.

Inside Gwynn and Travers met again for the first time in many years.

'Congratulations, Gwynn, as decadent a choice as only you could make.'

The fabric of most of the chairs and banquettes had been slit and the dun-coloured walls were pitted.

'I like the place, it reminds me of my Fitzrovia days.'

This was manifestly unreasonable, as Travers must have realized. Unless he was prepared to imagine a ten-year-old Gwynn hobnobbing with the boozy melancholics of that hopeful, hapless imploded culture.

'But you've prospered since then?'

It was less of a question than a mocking accusation. Gwynn could not remember ever liking Travers. On the couple of occasions they had had dealings with each other Travers, in spite of being his junior by a good decade, had turned him into a needy lickspittle. There was something about the man that, in spite of his wish and intention, made him feel and act like a submissive whore.

'Hardly thriving, but at least I'm master of my own sinking ship.'

His declaration of proud but impecunious independence once uttered immediately struck him as distastefully pathetic.

'So I've heard. I gather a gainful commission would not be unacceptable.'

There were only two other customers in the horseshoe-shaped bar. One, now a hamburger and hot-dog pedlar, was known to Gwynn as a former slasher on Albert Diamond's staff when that gentleman ran Soho. The other, an elderly Eurasian tart, was opulently decked out in mauve and gold.

'Recession has hit the arts particularly hard.'

Two barmen with faces the colour of fresh cement polished glasses with soiled towels. They exuded the keen attentiveness of professional mourners at a pauper's interment.

'What – or perhaps I should say who – is your particular forte now? I seem to remember that last time we did business it was Edward Seago.'

'I like to think that whatever I put my hand to gives satisfaction.'

He hated sounding like an obsequious second-rate tailor; it was the effect of Travers' bulgy face beaming at him.

'I suppose you've been flooding the market with Picassos?'

'Actually, I've been quite quiet of late. Doing my own thing, you might say.'

In a corner, an old and hyperinsensitive jukebox played relentlessly without ever being fed. Its volume compelled them both to talk more loudly than either wished.

'That's probably just as well. I don't like and I don't need this sort of business and if there's too much unrecorded stuff flying around it smells. To be blunt, I'm only doing this because you're a friend of Briar's sister and ... well, for old time's sake, I suppose.'

Gwynn knew that this was his cue for apologies and fulsome gratitude. He delivered both. He saw that Travers' glass was empty. It was typical of Travers to order Campari and Punt-e-Mes in such a patently unassuming pub and it was typical of Travers that he got it. He waited at the bar while the barman apparently washed up all of the previous night's glasses.

In a way the delay was a godsend, for it gave Gwynn time to consider how much, if anything, Travers knew about several works that he had passed off on a member of the Lingfield family some years ago. Knowing Travers' relish for intrigue and scandal, it was unlikely that he could avoid alluding to the matter even if he had only the meagrest suspicion. On the other hand, if he was clever and said nothing, his own impulse to ask him outright what he knew would be immense but must be resisted. It was uncanny how the past returned; how could he possibly have guessed all that time ago that he would ever come across a member of the Lingfield family again, let alone be living with one. On the whole he felt safe; if the pictures had been detected he would surely have heard of it from Crécy. And if Travers had seen them, which was not impossible, it by no means followed that he would have doubted their authenticity and then tumbled to their origin. It gave Gwynn a small but invigorating pleasure to despise the bright cherry that adorned Travers' glass.

'Sorry about the hiatus.'

'Gwynn, I've been thinking about where we ought to go from here.'

'Yes?'

He watched Travers suck the cherry from its cocktail stick and then with gusto slowly chew it. If he were ever to paint Travers' portrait, he would place a rosy cherry between his lips, rather in the manner of Caravaggio. Travers pressed his hands together and rested his chin on the tips of his fingers – an innocent might have thought him at prayer.

'I'm no businessman but if I were, I suppose I would say that first we must identify our market and secondly create a product for it.'

He paused, perhaps he expected an ovation. Gwynn was in no position to deny him anything, so he grunted assent.

'The market's radically changed since your day, the English collectors have all but vanished and the Americans are dormant, so your dreamy eighteenth and nineteenth-century landscapes are strictly for the birds.'

This was getting close to the bone. But there was no hint of insinuation or complicity in Travers' expression. Gwynn sought comforting distraction in fingering a chalk lump in his left ear lobe.

'The new collectors in London, the ones with money, are the exiles: the Lebanese, quite a few panicky Chinese, the odd Greek and one or two South Africans. They're mostly *nouveaux riches* and are perfectly happy to be told what they should like, providing of course they're all told the same thing.'

Gwynn wondered whether Travers saw the funny side of this and decided that he didn't and couldn't. A complete lack of sense of humour was one of his more lamentable defects. If one became what one ate, why shouldn't one equally become those whom one fed? Travers' disdain for the people he so unscrupulously supplied and who, in turn, so richly rewarded him was a self-deceiving ruse, for he was as much a part of their philistine and hedonistic world as they were.

'So, we're talking about people like Rothko, early Derain, Matisse, even Frank Stella. Could you manage any of them?'

Gwynn suddenly felt flattered, even though it was thanks to Travers. He was convinced he couldn't do Rothko, principally because he despised him. He felt pretty good about Derain and Matisse, though their apparent simplicity was dangerously deceptive. As for Stella, wasn't he still alive?

'How much, Travers?'

'Who do you want to do?'

'Perhaps a Derain and a twenties, thirties Matisse interior. I'll do some preliminary studies, of course.'

A glow spread gradually over Travers' face. He had the look of a once broody hen hearing the cracking of the shell of her first chick.

'I think that sounds good.'

'What about the money? Crécy's desperate to live in Tuscany.'

It was pleasant to have reached this stage of the proceedings; he now knew that Travers needed him. Well, if not precisely that, at least accepted that because Gwynn's products had market potential, they could be of service to each other. It was also pleasant to reflect on the quaintness of the complex relationship: Briar and Travers, himself and Crécy. Presumably Briar was Travers' uncommonly close friend, if so both he and Travers were involved with the same family. It was almost as though they were brothers-in-law. The whole set-up was deliciously, wickedly tangy.

'I don't want to be a bore, but how much were you thinking of, Travers?'

'Good point. Glad you brought it up.'

Travers produced a smart black leather notepad and on it

scribbled some figures with a sleek gold fountain pen. From time to time his face contracted in a wrinkled agony of concentration. He relaxed briefly.

'By the way, you're right about Stella, there's an obvious and intrinsic risk in creating works by extant artists.'

He totted up numbers. His lips twitched. He screwed up his eyes. It was all done in the finest tradition of amateur dramatics, for he'd worked out the sums to a T days ago. It was quite simple. Gwynn would get ten per cent of the negotiated price. He put the top on his pen and allowed his face to soften and wax. He smiled brightly at his talent.

'Yes, Gwynn, I think you'll be pleasantly surprised, very pleasantly surprised indeed.'

'Don't tease. How much?'

'Before I tell you, I think it's only fair to point out that my expenses in orchestrating the transactions will be enormous. There'll be travel, entertainment ... '

Travers' expression was earnestly sincere: that of a saintly evangelist.

'... a very great deal of entertainment indeed, the odd sweetener for expert authentification, and that can be jolly expensive. Then there's the cost of documentary evidence of provenance. As you can appreciate, it all adds up. And don't forget that with two products – sorry, two works of art – that's likely to mean two separate transactions and so double the expenses.'

He beamed beatifically, for now he was approaching the happy dénouement.

'None the less, in spite of the very heavy operational expenditure, you can be sure of between ten and twenty thousand pounds a picture. Now what do you think of that?'

He sat back defiantly, radiating avuncular indulgence, a veritable Mr Lillyvick. Gwynn, on the other hand, looked uncertain, reflective. Travers waited for him to say something. His impatience was fringed with altruism and generosity, the combination was hard on the facial muscles.

'Yes, Travers, I think that sounds pretty fair. Incidentally, you haven't mentioned your commission.'

Travers couldn't believe his ears.

'How stupid of me. I believe ten per cent is the customary rate.'

Gwynn nodded his head knowingly. In spite of his reticence he was inwardly overwhelmed by the riches that Travers was proffering him. Between twenty and forty thousand pounds, less a piffling commission. It was an unimaginable sum. His insides felt as if they were swimming in champagne, he was as light-headed as a rollicking calf, he wanted to bellow with laughter. He clenched his teeth to preserve his outward sang-froid. Tonight Crécy and he would dine off oysters and lobster and Krug. Tuscany was no longer a dream, it was as real as his present circumstances were drab and sordid.

Travers, too, had achieved and sustained a look of bored piety while all the time jubilant thoughts teemed and exploded in his head. He found it hard to keep still; his fingers, out of sight under the table, skipped and gambolled ceaselessly, he jiggled his legs like a small boy anxious to go out. Over three hundred and fifty thousand! Soon the luscious Renoir, so often dangled before his tantalized eyes by Wildenstein, could be his. How he longed to see Wildenstein's face.

'What about another drink to celebrate our compact?'

'Just a quick one then, I've got to be getting along.'

With barely disguised irritation they exchanged banal inconsequences, swigged their drinks and acted like grave, jaded businessmen at the day's end.

'Bumped into Guy Cooper the other night, do you remember him?'

'Right now I should be at the Zabdanis' do. Oh well, life's too short. Ha ha ha!'

Each wanted to leave so that he could revel in his own fortune and relish his scorn for the other. But, like unsatisfied lovers longing to break apart, neither wished to be the first to do so.

Chapter Eighteen

BRIAR let it be known generally that he lived in a garret, but it was not, strictly speaking, the humble abode he would have had people believe. His flat was the old nursery suite on the top floor of Terrick House.

He lay on his back under a primrose silk sheet unable to sleep. Next to the bedroom was his dressing-room and beyond that a bathroom furnished with bidet and hip-bath. A small sitting-room-cum-study overlooked the garden at the back. In the old days tugs and boats hooted on the river. Now the sound was of lorries and cars on the Embankment, a muffled, soporific murmur through the double-glazing.

Briar could not sleep because he was enduring a rare but periodic bout of self-repugnance. At such times he was alien to himself, as if he were viewing his being through the mind of another, or as if his ego, psyche and sexuality had all been turned on their heads. Indeed, in this mood he particularly detested what he considered were the feminine elements of his character: his passiveness, his sensibility, his acquiescence – even his swarthy, sensitive looks.

His room glowed with the orangey-roseate light of the night sky. In a corner was stacked a pyramid of soft toys; some were relics of childhood, others were more recently acquired. On the walls, dimly visible, were posters: three androgynous Beardsley creatures, a largely naked Mishima pierced by arrows in the manner of St Sebastian, and Paddington Bear – pot of marmalade in one hand, suitcase in the other. Had he felt less paralytically diffident he would have sprung from the bed and snatched them from the walls.

Travers was largely to blame for his state of despairing humiliation. Travers knew how much he depended on him, yet for days he'd heard nothing from him. He had repeatedly tried to ring him, but there was never an answer. He could imagine Travers sitting near the telephone listening to its ringing and, knowing who it would be, not picking it up. Travers could be very cruel. God, that was exactly the sort of word he hated himself for using. It sounded so limp and self-pitying. He shut his eyes; he would picture himself performing an act of such bravado that everyone – his family, his friends, but especially Travers – would be astounded. Yomping across the Falklands was *passé*; he'd done it too often, it had degenerated into a doddle. An *affaire de cœur* with Princess Diana had its possibilities, but suffered from basic implausibility and might all too easily develop into a far from heroic farce. Avowals of passion splashed worldwide, 'What is a queen's throne to me compared with my love for this man?' Shades of Tristan, it was altogether too risky. He thought of Bel.

He had invited himself to tea with her a week ago. Tea had seemed the right meal to suggest, and when he arrived he saw that he had chosen wisely. A round table in the middle of her tiny living-room was spread with mustard-and-cress sand-wiches, Marmite-and-lettuce sandwiches, an uncut loaf of wholemeal bread and pots of peanut butter, honey and strawberry jam. In the centre stood a very dark and large chocolate cake. Clearly she was of a generation that believed that tea was a meal that mattered, or perhaps she had forgotten that he was no longer ten. All had gone swimmingly; he had eaten like a ravenous colt, appreciated the paintings in a guileless way and left full of his great-aunt's blessing and the conviction that it would not be long before she penned a codicil to her will. In fact – he was almost certain he hadn't imagined it subsequently – as he was shutting her door he had seen her flit across the room towards her fussily ornate ormolu desk.

To kill her, or on second thoughts, to put her to sleep – there was nothing to be gained from using unneces-sarily emotive language – would unquestionably be an act of great bravado, an awfully big adventure. He remembered what Travers had said about the needy man who had dispatched his own mother: he had done it 'very humanely and very swiftly', and 'he had never suffered the slightest remorse'. Briar wondered whether any of it was true. The trouble with Travers – actually, it was one of his most engaging traits – was that he had a fiendish sense of humour, added to which he was a master of deceit. But, just supposing ...

Outside there was a dull thump followed by the squealing of many brakes and then a gradual fading of sound. Unwholesome curiosity drew Briar from his bed as shameful contempt for his possessions had failed to do. He stood by the window in his Cambridge-blue nightshirt and looked below. It was hard to discern clearly what had happened. A lorry and its trailer at right angles to the road blocked all four lanes, a car appeared to be half under the driver's cabin and what might have been a bicycle lay on the pavement. He climbed back into bed excitedly awaiting the exhilarating cacophony of sirens.

He prided himself on his high conscience threshold; he considered it rather Greek, or Spartan or something. It made him impervious to all but the grossest reproaches. He had acquired and developed the quality at school. He justified it in moral terms as making the most of free will. If he did enter the Church, and it increasingly appeared to him as a career in which his talents would be squandered, it was a talent he wanted to elaborate as his own particular contribution to Christian revelation. With a thrill he heard the wails of approaching sirens. He could make out a fire-engine and the shriller sound of a police car. He wondered if the ambulance would come in time.

He believed in sin. The common mistake was that it should be spurned. This belief made a mockery of Christ's incarnation and redeeming crucifixion. If man rejected sin, then the Cross became purposeless because the only reason Christ died was to save man from the consequences of his sins. Not to sin was therefore an infernally presumptuous rejection of God's sacrifice.

But murder? And particularly someone he really quite liked. But every day men shed the blood of every kind of living creature. Only God restricted himself to self-sacrifice. And, after all, the act would be relative to the magnitude of the reward: the means of a life of comfort and ease. If only the victim were his father, a man who was no use to himself or anyone else, and who was half dead in any case.

90

Briar had paid him a call in hospital the other day. In spite of being stuck in a ghastly, common ward, he had looked surprisingly well, perhaps a bit pale and thin in the cheeks. They hadn't had much to say; they never had. His father, without a whiff of prompting, had proudly talked of his treatment. How he was wheeled into a square room and then left alone while his purple-marked body was subjected to radiation. And how the staff had peered at him through portholes in the walls and made him feel like a previously unrecorded sub-species of fish. Then they had sat in silence until he was just about to go, when his father had introduced him to a whole lot of bedridden proles whom he had ludicrously but emphatically described as his friends. It had been a relief to get out into the fresh air. But that pleasure had been tempered by the sight of his reflection in a shop window, a reminder that he'd been sired in his father's likeness.

Bel. If he did have the guts to remove her, it would have to be done in a way that nobody could conceivably link with him. It would have to look like the work of a madman. He thought of a case in France years ago. It had been vividly described in a book of vicious murders he had bought when the subject fascinated him. He had formed quite a library. Two demure, half-witted sisters had butchered their employee and her daughter. The victims' heads had resembled blood puddings; their thighs had been as liberally notched as a baguette and their gouged eyes scattered like marbles. He wondered if he was up to it. As a child, aimless in the kitchen, he had watched his mother skinning a hare; when she had finished, she'd held it up, and it had looked like a shiny, blood-smeared baby.

He turned over. Sleep was inaccessible; plotting concentrated the mind all too wonderfully. He would feel awful the next day. There was probably some truth in the nanny adage that the hours of sleep before midnight were twice as beneficial as those after. Outside, the tumult from the accident went on. And then with a start that flung his head sideways, he remembered Francis. He too would have to go. He didn't care for the beady-eyed, chattering creature, but the prospect of having to destroy him was chilling. God, it was turning into a massacre.

Chapter Nineteen

A man in a dark suit stood in the doorway; pessimistically he looked from bed to bed. He carried a bunch of flowers wrapped in paper, he held it ineptly as if he wanted no part of it, a vegan saddled with a carcass. Then with a start of recognition he waved bashfully at Bliss. With curiosity Bliss watched the dapper figure pick his way down the ward occasionally offering a nervous smile to an inmate. He was practically upon him before Bliss recognized Simon.

'Hello, old man, you look flourishing.'

Simon beamed down at the pallid, dull-eyed patient and dropped the flowers on to the bed-table.

'I thought I'd come in person rather than telephone, though hospitals give me the willies.'

'It's good of you to come.'

Bliss shrank down in the bed, he couldn't imagine to what hideous misfortune Simon's presence was owed. Before his appearance he'd been thinking about pain and fear. For thirty years he had forgotten what they felt like. He knew he had experienced both at school, but after that he hadn't, until now, had the opportunity of savouring them in full measure.

'You've been much missed. By the way do they mind if one smokes?'

Simon produced a cheroot and, there being no chair, sat on the edge of the bed.

'You'll never guess who I saw at the Colmores'.'

Bliss shook his head feebly.

'Mazda Renault. Do you remember, you were rather keen about her, she was that bird that used to piss standing up?'

Surely Simon hadn't travelled halfway across town to tell him this.

'Oh, and Dodo and Phiz Polar gave a marvellous house-warming. You know they've bought the Mellinks' place? It's that house right on the river.'

Bliss watched the ascension of heavy blue smoke from the cheroot and wondered if anyone would complain.

'So when are they going to let you out? We'll have a celebratory party, I should think you could do with a bit of a thrash.'

He couldn't think of anything he wanted less. He had discovered that fear was crueller than pain. He was more than halfway through the treatment and the knowledge that in a matter of days he would be thrust from his cocoon of camaraderie and dependence was an abiding, aching fear. His burns, his exhaustion, his nausea were tormenting but endurable. It was the future he could not bear.

'I imagine I'll have to take it easy to begin with.'

Simon tapped ash on to a saucer on which an untouched cup of tea stood. He lowered his voice, like a penitent about to touch on his worst sin.

'Incidentally, I'm as sorry as you must be that we had to sell so low. I didn't want to make a big song and dance about it at the time, particularly as you were about to come in here.'

He brightened and his voice resumed its slightly louder than necessary tone.

'Of course, looking on the bright side, it does mean that we can put the loss against any future gain.'

A splay-footed black woman, in a lurid green overall, with great dignity and leisure pushed round a trolley and collected cups and saucers. She said nothing, she might have been alone in the room.

'I dare say the food's filthy. Can't think why you didn't insist on a private room.'

Simon leaned forward and again dropped his voice. His breath smelled of good living.

'There is another thing. I don't want to upset you unduly, but do you get to see the F.T. here?'

Bliss smiled and then laughed, it was a sublimely fatuous idea. Simon looked hurt, even shocked.

'I wondered if you'd been following Cleanands. It's holding steady, but I was hoping for something better. It's all tied up with the runaway bull market on Wall Street. Of course, time's still on our side.'

Bliss didn't really care what happened to Cleanands or whether he became a pauper and was put in the poor-house. (Though on second thoughts he was pretty sure that that admirable institution was no more.) In the end, and merciful heaven the end couldn't be far away now, the *Financial Times* and Simon and the bulls and bears and stags and Cleanands could all go to hell as far as he was concerned. It was because of an enduring loyalty to Simon that he tried to look anxious.

'So what is Cleanands at?'

'It's improved since you sold.'

'But insufficiently for my call.'

There was an irony there that Bliss couldn't be bothered to point out.

'Actually, Bliss, what I really want to suggest, and that is why I've come here personally because I do see that it concerns us both and there is still, thank God, such a thing as personal responsibility ... '

He had run out of direction or words or both. He sucked long and ruminatively on his cheroot.

'What I mean is that temporarily, and I can't over-emphasize that it is just temporarily, we think of letting your house for a spell. I can arrange a service flat for you so you wouldn't have to worry about a thing. We'd – that is to say, you'd get a decent bit of income from the let, and you'd be able to convalesce without the bother of housekeeping. What do you think?'

Simon arose from the bed to underline the wisdom of his suggestion and the conclusion of his visit. It was a godsend that Bliss had said he'd need to take it easy for a bit, otherwise he'd never have thought of introducing convalescence into his counsel.

'Do what you like, Simon. Oh, and don't forget your usual commission on anything you handle.'

Simon looked down on his stricken client and despised him. He realized he always had. Ever since he'd first met him (at a house cricket match, as he remembered it), Bliss had played the role of listless aristocrat consummately and now, on his deathbed, he was still doling out charity. Some bloody charity; the man was beggared.

Chapter Twenty

BY deception, Lady Lingfield had gained admission to Dr Israel's consulting-room.

'Lady Lingfield, you have no more right to ask me that than you have to be here. You are wasting my time and I must ask you to leave.'

'Naughty me!'

She smiled mischievously. Her podgy fists sparkled with jewels. She sat on the edge of the chair and thrust her peach-blown face at the doctor imploringly. She was confident that her allure was irresistible.

'Please, Lady Lingfield, don't make me lose my temper. I have patients waiting outside.'

'But Doctor, he is my only child. He is the only sane relative I have left. All I am asking is that you tell me what hope there is for him.'

She snapped open her black handbag and took out an intricately lacy handkerchief that was more lacunae than material. It was the last of a set that had belonged to her mother. It came from Valenciennes, she only used it at times of distress.

'Ask your son. I have been completely open with him. He knows his prognosis.'

'You have no idea how much he dislikes upsetting his mother. He cherishes me, he really does; why, it was only by chance I found out he wasn't well. Ever since my husband, Hubert ... '

She dangled the lace handkerchief under her nose and cast her eyes down to the last button of the doctor's waistcoat.

' ... I've become utterly dependent on my boy, and then there is the burden of my wretched brother, like a child he is, poor lamb. He should be in a home, but who could do that to one of their own? Bliss does so much for him.'

'Lady Lingfield, much as I would like to, I can do no more for your son than I have.'

'So it's as I feared. How long, Doctor, how long?'

She blew busily into her handkerchief; when she got home she would wash it gently in Lux.

Dr Israel abominated such situations; the terminally ill were always so much braver, less self-absorbed than their families.

'Your son is clearly a very sensible and capable person. I have no doubt that he will make the necessary arrangements to ensure that his loved ones are cared for. It's a pity we can't all share his courage.'

'But months, Doctor, or years?'

She clutched her handkerchief in one hand and with both held on to her handbag as if it might at any moment float away.

'Not more than six, and probably less than three. I'm talking about months.'

She bolted upright, genuinely shocked.

'How can you say that so callously? It's like a death sentence.'

The handkerchief fluttered to the floor. Without it she was abandoned. She made odd movements with her arms, like someone ineffectually learning to swim.

Dr Israel rolled a pen up and down his blotter and wondered whether he had unintentionally committed an indiscretion. He wanted to be with his wife and daughter in the dense and inviolable protection of his home. He did not want to be pestered by a moneyed, spoilt and neurotic goy.

'I have told your son to talk with me any time he feels the need to.'

Lady Lingfield shrivelled into herself. Her face puckered and she drew her handbag into her stomach as if it were a foundling.

'Do you have children, Doctor?'

'I have a daughter.'

She made herself comfortable and moistened her lips. Her mouth quivered like a wasp's bottom in anticipation of stinging. She enunciated with deliberation.

'Cosset her, Doctor, and count yourself blessed that you

have not suffered the ultimate sorrow: the loss of your own flesh and blood.'

Dr Israel said nothing. With the tip of his tongue he stroked a spot on his gum. He rang a bell and let his eyes rest on the row of pebbles on the mantelshelf.

In the dining-hall of Lingfield Place Reverend Mother Euberta addressed the assembled Little Sisters of St Luke. They sat at refectory tables as neat and docile as dolphins.

'Dear Sisters in Christ, our prayers for Lord Lingfield have not yet been answered. But that does not mean that they will not be. It means that we must pray ever more strenuously. Our dear friend and benefactress, Miss Lingfield, telephoned me this morning with the unhappy news that her nephew is now considered by his doctor to be terminally ill.'

Sister Pelagia, the oldest member of the Order and a woman who valued strict regularity highly, tried in vain to stifle a groaning rumble in her stomach.

'But, for God nothing is impossible. He gave us prayer and the power of prayer is therefore infinite. We have asked the humanly impossible of Him before and He has answered our prayers. Some would say miraculously.'

Sister Pelagia closed her eyes better to concentrate on a miracle for Lord Lingfield and to shut out the cutlery and platter that lay untouched, immaculate before her. She tried to remember what Lord Lingfield looked like, she had only seen him once or twice.

'Some of you may be wondering why I am making such an issue of Lord Lingfield when we have so many sick and dying to pray for. It is partly because he is a comparatively young man and partly because were it not for his family we would not be here now. And though he has not visited us frequently he has, I know, held us dear in his heart.'

Sister Pelagia suddenly remembered that it was Wednesday and that meant Irish stew and dumplings with those delightful grains of pearl barley.

'And so, dear Sisters, remember "All shall be well, and all shall be well, and all manner of thing shall be well." '

And afterwards, thought Sister Pelagia, there would be nutmeg-flavoured junket.

Bel joined a queue in Sloane Street waiting for a 137 bus. A plump woman dressed in a diversity of mauves and dragged down by plastic bags, and a shrunken man with a lopsided watery eye stood there. She bearded the woman immediately.

'Are you a Christian? I mean, do you believe in the power of prayer?'

The plump woman showed no surprise but merely placed a reflective forefinger on her chin.

'Of course, dear, deep down everybody does. But why do you want to know?'

'It's my nephew. Young middle-aged. Lung cancer and a very poor outlook. But I do believe if enough people batter on God's door, He has to listen. Sort of spiritual artillery bombardment. His name is Bliss. I am grateful.'

The watery-eyed man had half turned away, too cowardly to confront Bel, too diffident to walk away.

'And you, will you pray for my nephew?'

'I can't promise anything.'

'It'll take you less than a minute morning and night.'

'Well, I'll have to ask the wife.'

A 137 drew up. Shamelessly Bel sprang on first and took a banquette seat. Next to her sat a young man entirely clad in black. His brilliantly-coloured hair was dressed in the manner of the Hurons. She clutched one of his silver-studded leather lapels and drew him to her.

'Young man, I want you to pray for a miracle for my nephew.'

'Sure, lady, whatever you say.'

Bel knew then that Bliss would be all right.

Chapter Twenty-One

SIMON had been as good as his word. He had made arrangements for Bliss's house to be rented to an American couple with two small children for a minimum of six months and a maximum of a year. And he had found him a service flat ('a compact, bachelor's *pied-à-terre*') in a large, modern block within easy walking distance of his mother.

The flat was on the eighth floor. Bliss was sitting on one of two easy chairs. None of the furniture was his own. He didn't know how long he'd been sitting there but it was still daylight. The room was insulated from outside sound and the only noises came from his wristwatch and his decrepit breathing.

There was a bookcase but there were no books in it, instead a unit that contained a digital clock, a radio, a cassette player and a television. Bliss had not yet discovered how they worked. Behind the bookcase lay the kitchenette. The bathroom with *en suite* lavatory was by the front door. He had found that both doors could not be open at the same time. The only window was in the bed-sitting-room and it was sealed.

He saw few people, but that was partly because he discouraged visitors, they wearied him. He had noticed, though, that certain people – particularly his contemporaries and the young – shunned him as if cancer were as contagious as the plague. Simon continued to ring him daily with a market report he no longer took in and expectations he no longer believed in. Sometimes an ambulance came to take him for a check-up at the hospital, and every day a Filipina appeared to make his bed and to dust. She smiled incessantly. He had given up making lists, there was nothing to put down.

His last list lay on a glass-topped coffee table that straddled most of the room. His final entry under Pleasures was

'Tilbury'; that under Regrets was 'Death of John'. He'd added nothing since his departure from the hospital.

When the room became so dark that it was time to turn the lights on, Bliss got ready for bed. It was a happy moment, he folded up his day clothes, put on a pair of coarse, woolly pyjamas, ate a biscuit and drank a glass of milk, and knew that though he might not sleep much the hours of darkness were an escape from the harsh dolour of the day.

He would like to have said a prayer or two, but could remember none save 'Jesus, tender shepherd hear me' which no longer seemed apt.

The heat in the air-conditioned room was specially unpleasant at night. He lay under a single sheet and reminded himself that the less movement he made the more comfortable he would be.

He didn't fear death, or even its process. There would be no pain. John had been chocked up to the eyeballs with drugs before he died. What appalled him was life, and it was a natural irony that he should have only discovered this when he was at the end of it. The knowledge of his complete loneliness and insignificance would have been unbearable without the promise of death. But as he was not yet dead, the harsh truth preyed upon him continually, stripping him of the last, minutest morsels of his human vanity. The past, present and future were one single fatuity. 'Dust thou art: and unto dust shalt thou return.' It was perplexing and shocking that Christians with all their cant about immortality should none the less utter and believe such an unequivocal declaration of extinction. But life after death was an infinitely terrible prospect. As a boy, he had often lain in bed unable to sleep and petrified by the thought of living for ever. He still found the notion horrifying: for ever and a day, and after that for ever.

His detachment surprised him. He wondered why it didn't dismay him that he would never make love to a woman again, never bring down a high-flying pheasant or enjoy the first spring crocuses in the park. But he was half dead, and too bloody tired to want anything but release.

At school he'd had to learn a poem in which there was a couplet he could still remember.

And when you look back it's all like a puff,
Little and over, and short enough.

It was silly of people to doubt that a drowning man would
have time to see his whole life pass before him. His own would
take a couple of seconds. Childhood in the country, school,
more school, army, affairs, marriage, gambling, children,
affairs, divorce, more affairs, cancer. And out of it all no great,
abiding love, no undying friendship. That was the stuff of
fiction. Not really anybody he even respected, except possibly,
and it only now occurred to him, Dr Israel, about whom he felt
peculiarly ambivalent: the man simultaneously fascinated and
repelled him.

Even if he had been allotted a longer lifespan there was no
reason to suppose that the future would have been any more
rewarding than the past. Less, in all probability: a crescendo of
disappointments and impoverishments climaxing in utter
desolation. He wondered if he was verging towards self-pity.

The telephone rang. Its sudden jangle in the silent, dark
room was alarming. He would not have been surprised by a
summons from Charon.

'Lord Lingfield? It's David Israel. Shall we dispense with
surnames? I wonder if you would care to dine one night? It'll
just be family, not a party.'

So unexpected was the invitation that Bliss accepted it
without hesitation; a decision that he immediately regretted.

101

Chapter Twenty-Two

TRAVERS' flat was a cramped ivory tower at the end of several flights of stairs, but the address could hardly have been bettered. The cachet of Belgravia more than compensated for any breathlessness.

Gwynn arrived puffing and bearing a cumbersome portfolio.

'How very exciting! I am all agog. What will you have to drink, Gwynn?'

The immediate impression on entering the drawing-room was that this was the house of a man of taste, albeit florid. The chartreuse green walls were lined from hip level to ceiling with paintings and drawings and the gold of their ornate frames was reflected in the heavy damask curtains. On occasional tables were strewn *objets d'art* and above the mantelshelf a giltwood oval mirror glittered. The room had featured in a magazine devoted to the art of interior decoration. It required a fastidious eye to discern that much of the splendour was meretricious, that many of the pictures were trivial and the furniture largely spurious.

'Well, it certainly looks as if you've come up in the world.'

Travers didn't care for this observation and overlooked it.

'Are you satisfied with your labours?'

Travers was determined that Gwynn should remember the hierarchy of their relationship.

'I'm reserving judgment until I've heard what you think.'

Gwynn sat on the edge of a sofa and placed the portfolio on the floor in front of him. It was large and black and leatherette. He opened it with the infuriating protraction of a magician.

'First the Derain.'

Gwynn placed a sheet of thick paper about two foot by three on a low table. Travers bent over it and glared at it.

'But it's on paper!'

'Never mind the material, what about the picture?'

A jade green River Thames swished past a monumental, smoky blue St Paul's. In the foreground a motley of freighters, tugs and lighters jostled: a dazzling fleet of scarlet, cadmium, violet and cobalt.

'For Christ's sake, why did you use paper?'

'Notice the signature.'

Gwynn pointed to the bottom left corner of the painting and indicated the signature composed entirely of small letters with a backward curving d.

'Great. But why paper for God's sake?'

'It's French, it's contemporary and, of course, as you well remember most of Derain's Fauve oils were painted on paper. An esoteric touch of verisimilitude, I'm sure you'll agree. Or perhaps you haven't handled much of his Fauve work?'

'Is that true?'

'Naturally. And now for the Matisse.'

Gwynn returned the river scene to the portfolio and scattered three sheets of sketches across the table with the deft assurance of a card-sharp.

'They're beautiful, simply beautiful, I congratulate you, Gwynn, you're a genius. And we can easily get rid of these.'

Travers pointed to the pin holes in the corners of the sheets.

'Don't. On no account must you touch them. They are the seals of authenticity. Matisse invariably pinned his paper to a board when drawing. Now for the finished product.'

Gwynn swept aside the sketches and reverently laid a canvas on the table. A featureless-faced girl in a long, swirling white gown sat on a rose-pink floor. Beside her squatted a cabriole-legged chair upholstered in canary yellow. An open window looked out on to a balcony dotted with pots of bright flowers, beyond lay a hyacinth sea.

'God, I can almost smell the air. I don't know how you do it, it's practically better than the real thing.'

'It is the real thing.'

'Show me the Derain again.'

Both paintings were placed side by side on the table.

'They hum, they sing. One is jazz, the other is Debussy. Heavens, you know I'm worried now that they're too good.'

103

But Travers was grinning and squeezing his clasped hands between his thighs.

'They are far and away the best things you've ever done. What's the date of the Matisse?'

'Late thirties, early forties. It's up to you, I haven't dated it, but I can. Actually it would be proper, he generally did.'

'And we'll keep those pin holes in the paper, those precious God-damned pin holes.'

'And about money, Travers? In all conscience I don't think I can let you have these without a fairly sizeable advance.'

'Of course, of course.'

It was funny because, beforehand, Gwynn had worried that Travers might find the pictures unsatisfactory, or might claim they were. And then there would have been an unholy to-do about the price or, like a rebuked schoolboy, he would have been sent home to do them again. But now that they were so clearly a success he felt no soaring relief or exuberance, just a quiet pride of the sort that an artisan might feel at a job well done.

'Cash or cheque? Obviously I can't give you cash straight away.'

'A cheque will be fine. How much were you thinking of?'

Travers had already whetted the appetites of a good many of his expatriate collector friends to the point of craving. He suspected that he could have sold the paintings to any one of them unseen. And now, as they were so much better than he had dared hope, he felt confident that there would be little objection if he nudged the price up by a hundred thousand apiece. However, there was no need for Gwynn to be troubled with these tiresome commercial details.

'I know you'll think two thousand sounds mean, but as you'll appreciate, where your work ends, mine begins and, of course, at this stage I'm hampered by cash-flow problems and the need to maintain a hefty float for the inevitable expenses.'

Gwynn nodded his head but he was thinking of Crécy. Naturally, she knew something was afoot, several times in the studio she had watched him at work, and said 'Gosh, that's super' and winked at him, but she could have no idea of the shoals of wealth he was about to land. He wondered if now that he was no longer impoverished, she would adore him even more. It was magical how he had become infected with her youthful optimism, her boisterous vitality, her *joie de vivre*. He remembered with an inward smile that he had once considered dropping her. The conceit of middle age!

'I quite understand, Travers. If you could make the cheque payable to cash and then I can let you have the pictures back as soon as the cheque is honoured. Is that all right?'

'Eminently.'

South of the Euston Road and north of Bloomsbury Crécy sat in Gwynn's studio, pen in hand, scratching the back of her head. At the top of a sheet of drawing paper on her lap she had written 'Darling'. On the floor beside her a few essentials were packed in a plastic bag.

She was in a hurry because Rollo Saxmundham had promised to pick her up in an hour and that had been forty minutes ago. Rollo was sweet and rather rich and madly in love with her and good-looking in a romantic way. Somehow she couldn't say no to him.

Her pen hovered over the paper. She didn't want Gwynn to think she was leaving him because he was poor. She was the first to acknowledge that only the poor lived authentic lives. The only trouble with poverty was that it was monotonous.

Darling Rollo! She had known him for aeons. He used to write to her from Eton. The school crest on the back of the envelopes made her the envy of all the other girls at her school.

Nor did she want Gwynn to think she was leaving because she despised genteel poverty more than wealth. She had heard from her brother who had heard from Travers that Gwynn was going to be paid about thirty thousand pounds for the pictures and she had a horrible suspicion that he would think that real money. Poor, dear Gwynn! So naïve. Rollo made more than four times that a year.

She screwed up the paper and taking another sheet wrote swiftly and with assurance, 'I am going now while there is still time to get my life together. I sacrificed everything for you and all you did was ill-treat me. God may forgive you. I never will.'

She left the sheet on the broken-down sofa and smiling brightly stepped out of the house to greet Rollo who was awaiting her in his shining motor-car.

Chapter Twenty-Three

DAVID Israel picked Bliss up on his way home from hospital.

'So, how are things? What do you do with yourself all day?'

'I sleep a lot, or rather doze. If I go out I keep thinking I recognize people only to remember they're dead.'

'Don't worry, I've been doing that all my life.'

They drove northwards; after Lord's cricket ground Bliss was lost.

'I hope your wife likes chocolates. I've got her some.'

'Tell me a woman who doesn't.'

The traffic was slow, much of the driving aggressive and bad-tempered. The doctor was imperturbable but hardly spoke. Bliss contented himself with looking out of the window. Road after road of red brick houses, a cemetery, a stark, utterly unprepossessing hotel, a battlemented block of flats; it might have been another city. Perhaps it was, perhaps the good doctor was conducting him to the nether world.

'Do you live in London?'

'Why do you ask?'

'I was wondering how I was going to get home.'

'Don't worry, I'll drive you.'

'Oh, that's too much.'

Bliss's children when they were small used to sit in the back of the car interminably singing a two-note song whose lyrics were limited to 'Where are we going, why are we going?' For the first time the questions seemed reasonable. He wasn't apprehensive, just weary and perplexed. Why was an orthodox Jewish doctor entertaining his dying gentile patient in, of all places, the bosom of his family? Perhaps it was no odder than the dying gentile patient accepting the invitation.

'Is there anything special I should know?'

'How do you mean?'

'Well, am I expected to take my shoes off at the door and bow down before your wife? I'm sorry, that sounded rude.'

'You've never been in an orthodox home before?'

'Never.'

'You've never eaten kosher food before?'

'No.'

'Just be yourself, enjoy yourself and don't expect my womenfolk to laugh at smutty jokes.'

'And kosher food?'

'My wife is a good cook. I'm sure you'll enjoy her food.'

They were driving through the suburbs now, the houses were grand, detached; an exotica of myriad styles. A white, stuccoed villa pimpled with minarets was neighbour to a fussy amalgam of half a dozen of the châteaux of the Loire, which in turn was neighbour to a fortress-like cube of bronze-tinted glass and pink marble. Their opulence was brazen. None of them was protected by so much as a fence or even a hedge. Instead television cameras crowded their walls and entrances accusingly monitoring every angle of access.

'What sort of people live in these places?'

'Mostly Arabs.'

The traffic had thinned. From time to time the doctor hummed tunelessly.

'Tell me, is Bliss your real forename?'

'I was christened Arthur, my father was something of a Tennyson fan, but I've always been known as Bliss.'

'Do you mind if I call you Arthur?'

'Not at all, though I've always thought it rather an absurd name.'

'Compared with Bliss? Well, here we are.'

They turned off a quiet, tree-lined road and drove up a long, thickly-gravelled drive. Beyond a high privet hedge Bliss caught a glimpse of a low, steeply-roofed house.

'It looks like a ranch.'

'I like a house to be made of wood. Atavism, I suppose. Maybe something to do with the *shtetl* – sorry, the old villages our parents were brought up in.'

107

They went in. Once again, Bliss had the sensation that he was in a foreign land, but this time the impression was more forceful. The walls and the floor of the passage they walked down were of a gleaming, golden wood. There was an aromatic smell of beeswax polish and above and beyond that a curious smell, one of velvety warmth, a sort of chickeny savour. A very homey and soothing smell.

'Would you like to use the bathroom?'

'I'm fine.'

'Let me give you a drink and then, if you'll excuse me, I always like to freshen up when I get home.'

The door at the end of the passage opened into a wide, panelled room. Again there were the gleaming walls.

'Whisky or brandy?'

'Whisky would be lovely.'

'I'm sorry, perhaps you would prefer something else. For some unaccountable reason I feel it's the English thing to offer people whisky and brandy.'

The room and everything in it were inordinately clean. Bliss had the disconcerting impression that somebody must have left off dusting and polishing just before they entered.

'I won't be long.'

The silence was extraordinary and eerie. There was no sound of creaking floorboards, no muted conversation, no noises of preparation from the kitchen. He couldn't even hear his own movements as he explored the room, the sound of his footsteps were absorbed by the thick carpet. There was something else odd, but he couldn't at the moment detect what it was. A black grand piano loomed in one corner of the room, across it was draped a piece of filigreed embroidery that might once have been a clerical vestment. Through french windows Bliss looked out at a garden that was too orderly, too formal to be pleasing. On the walls were hung landscapes and seascapes in heavy gilt frames. The paintings were a shade too pristine. And then suddenly Bliss saw what was odd: there were no books in the room, not a solitary book.

'Here we are at last. Sorry to have left you alone.'

'I was admiring your pictures.'

They came in together. First the doctor, then his wife and his daughter. Mrs Israel was plump and dark-haired and she

108

wore a shiny emerald-green dress that drew attention to the greyness of her skin. She reminded Bliss of the peasant women he'd seen on service in Cyprus.

'Lord Lingfield, my wife, Miriam.'

It swiftly occurred to Bliss that Dr Israel might be a title snob and that that was the reason for the unexpected invitation. He hoped not: it would make the doctor less interesting. He turned to the daughter and was struck by the utter unsuitability of her long, frumpish, purple dress; it could only have been borrowed from her mother.

'Lord Lingfield, my daughter, Esther.'

She was short like her mother. But – and it was hard to tell – Bliss suspected that the hideous dress hid the body of a slender girl. She had mousy hair and freckled cheeks and a fairly pronounced beak. Bliss turned away from her, back to his hostess.

'Please call me Arthur.'

The two men caught each other's eye and smiled; it was an unfeigned and benign conspiracy.

'Well, Arthur, why don't we all sit down?'

In the middle of the room facing the french windows was an immense three-sided sofa; sitting on it they formed a square. Mother and daughter held tiny, floridly-cut glasses, the mother's fist was heavily armed with rings. A shaft of evening sunlight had fallen on a bed of red roses.

'The garden looks lovely at this time of year, don't you think?'

'I was admiring it before you came in. Do you do it all yourselves?'

Mrs Israel spluttered with pleasure.

'Oh, no, we don't have green fingers. Except, Esther, you grew some herbs in a pot once, didn't you?'

'Yes.'

'What sort were they, Esther?'

The girl darted a look at Arthur. He wondered if it was not done to address a girl of her faith directly. Her eyes were not unattractive, almost an amber colour.

'Lovage, you know, "There's rosemary, that's for remembrance; and there's lovage ... " that's for something else.'

'I've never heard of it.'

109

The girl perceptibly bridled. He wished he hadn't spoken, it had sounded as if he were impugning her.

'Are you planning on going away, Arthur?'

Mrs Israel revealed her own awareness of her slip by pursing her lips.

'I always leave things to the last moment, Mrs Israel.'

'Oh, you must call me Miriam.'

'Arthur, let me get you another whisky.'

Although the evening had so far presented Arthur with adequate grounds for boredom, embarrassment and scorn, he felt none of these emotions. To say that he was enjoying himself would have been going too far, but he was free of the frantic uneasiness that such an occasion would have caused him in the past. He ascribed it entirely to the doctor's calming presence.

'Do you have a garden?'

Esther couldn't bring herself to address him by name, asking the question had been enough to make her glower.

'Oh, no, I only have a tiny flat in central London, not even a window-box.'

'I thought perhaps you might have a family seat in the country.'

'I'm afraid that had to be sold long ago. It is now a convent, a home for pious Christian ladies.'

He knew he sounded idiotically patronizing, he was quite unable to help it. The plain girl in her unbecoming dress made him feel gentle. He wondered if she was a bit guileless.

'Do you speak in the House of Lords?'

'Oh, no, I'd have nothing to say.'

'What do you do?'

'Well, I used to do a bit of soldiering.'

'Come, Esther darling, too many questions. Shall we have dinner?'

Going to the dining-room Arthur vainly tried to imagine what drove the girl to ask her artless questions, when clearly to speak to him at all was agony. Unless it was puppy love. But that was absurd.

'Welcome, Arthur, to your first Jewish supper, may it not be your last.'

Arthur thought the toast tactless, blasphemous even, but the doctor beamed, so he beamed too, and everybody drank everybody's health in a sweetish white wine.

'Miriam, you tell Arthur what we are eating.'

'I thought, Arthur, as it was your first time, I would give you a typical meat. So we start with chopped chicken liver on rye bread with schmaltz. I hope you like it.'

'Schmaltz?'

The room was warm with a golden light that was reflected off the ubiquitous panelling, the brightly polished silver and the shining glassware. The table-setting would not have disgraced Ramillies, though Moyra would doubtless have complained that everything was modern and reproduction.

'Schmaltz is just chicken fat.'

Telling himself that it was no different from bread and dripping, a dish that Bel had treated him to in his youth, Arthur swallowed hard.

'A gentile colleague of mine was on a Swan's Hellenic cruise. One day the ship put in at Haifa and the holidaymakers were taken to a kibbutz restaurant for lunch.'

Moyra! What would she, or for that matter any of his friends think if they could see him now?

'On arrival, my colleague was asked "Meat or dairy?" to which he unwittingly replied "No, Swan's."'

Everyone laughed, but for the life of him Arthur couldn't think why.

'After supper, Arthur, when the ladies are not present, remind me to tell you the story of the American Jew and the moyl.'

If the doctor had been taciturn in his drawing-room, he was no conversational slouch in his dining-room.

'Oh, you may tell him now, David. After all, we are no longer children.'

Mrs Israel looked with voluptuous pride at her daughter.

Abruptly Arthur had the impression that there was or should have been a fifth person sitting at the table. He looked around it, but it was only set for four.

'I hope you enjoyed it. Next we have chicken soup with kneidlach. They are sort of meal dumplings.'

The room was getting warmer, it wasn't uncomfortable yet, but Arthur thought it a pity there were no windows. He had never suffered from claustrophobia, but could now understand how people did.

'Before I begin, I'd better explain, Arthur, that a moyl is a professional who performs the ritual circumcision of Jewish boys.'

It certainly was getting warmer. Arthur ran the back of his hand across his damp forehead. He was surprised the others hadn't noticed the change in temperature. He wondered whether it would be considered bad form if he asked if he could remove his jacket.

'So this American Jew is travelling across central Russia to visit the place where his parents came from. On the way his car breaks down in a tuppenny-ha'penny town. The garage tells him it will take half a day to mend, so in desperation he goes for a walk in this miserable place ...'

'A minute, David, I must bring on the next course. Esther, will you give me a hand?'

Arthur sipped his wine; though it was cold it made him hotter. He dabbed at his cheeks with his linen napkin and surreptitiously undid the top button of his shirt.

'Now, Arthur, for the main course we have fowl.'

'Sort of like chicken?'

It was an effort to speak, but he had to say something, he had been silent so long.

'The same. And with it we have horseradish sauce flavoured with beetroot, and on the side pickled dills. I know you'll like it.'

Arthur was beginning to understand the reason for the chickeny smell he'd first noticed on entering the house.

'All right if I continue? Fine. So the American Jew is going for a walk in this one-horse town and right on the edge of it where the fields begin he finds a shop with clocks and watches in the window. Good, he says to himself, I'll take the opportunity of having my watch regulated ... '

Arthur could barely eat, sweat streamed down his face on to his lips. His back felt as if it were on fire, his soaked shirt clung to his skin.

' ... and so he goes in and there at the back of the shop is a little old bearded man wearing a yarmulke – that, Arthur, is a Jewish skullcap. And the American Jew says to him ... '

Arthur suddenly realized who the missing person at the table was. He wondered how old the leukaemic son, the pebble boy, would have been now.

' ... "Would you look at my watch, please, it's running slow?" But the little old man pays him no attention and carries on reading an ancient and huge book.'

Arthur put down his knife and fork; he could no longer even make a pretence of eating. The heat in his back was now so great that the rest of his body seemed chilly, though sweat continued to run down his face. It was unimaginable that the others had noticed nothing, but they made no comment.

'So the American Jew, thinking the man is deaf, shouts at him, "My watch is slow, please fix it." But still the old man just goes on reading. By now the American Jew is fit to plotz – that, Arthur, means explode with anger. So he shakes the old man by the shoulder and roars at him, "Mend my watch!" '

Arthur felt sick with pain. His hands trembled. He'd never thrown up at table, he'd always dreaded it.

'Finally, the old man turns round and, speaking softly and with great dignity, says, "What makes you think I repair watches?" The American waves towards the front of the shop and yells, "All those clocks and watches!" '

An axe-head of molten steel embedded in his back. Arthur whispered, 'Lord, if I am dying, let me die now.'

'Wearily shaking his head the old man says, "I am a moyl, what would you have me put in the window?" '

There was laughter. It died the instant that Arthur's wineglass slipped from his hand and shattered on the table. Glazed, Arthur saw three white, anxious faces and heard a voice repeatedly enquiring,

'My God, was it the food?'

Chapter Twenty-Four

A stooped figure in tarnished armour was staggering through dense woodland, leaves the colour of copper fell before him. With the visor down he was half blind and from time to time he would lurch into a tree. The jangle of his battered armour made Esther wince. The going was heavy, each step seemed as if it must be his last. She wished that he would lift his visor so that she could see his face, but she could convey nothing to him. Now he was wading through swampland, his body was buffeted by gusts of oily mist that clung to his armour. Clumps of shoulder-high rushes hampered him. Swarms of thumb-sized and repulsive insects mobbed him. Esther caught snatches of piteous wailing. The sky was the colour of burnished steel, in its centre a sulphurous sun pulsated. Now the figure was on all fours, clawing through fine sand and making no headway. Clouds of dust scattered around him. Gradually he collapsed and turned on his back. Like a distressed beetle he flailed his limbs, lethargically, hopelessly. Esther looked closer and suddenly the steel visor flew open with the violence of a sprung trap. She peered into the black aperture: there was nothing inside but broken glass. She woke with a start.

Outside, it was raining steadily, a monotonous, reassuring sound. The house was silent. Esther wanted to know if Lord Lingfield was still under her roof. After his collapse he had been taken to her father's study and she had been sent to bed. For what had seemed an eternity she had lain awake dreading the wail of an ambulance before sleep had supervened. He was everything she'd long imagined a Lord would be: tall and dark and courteous. But for the hour and her parents, she would have looked to see if he was still in the house.

114

When a child she had been given, almost certainly by a mistake, an old book called *The Happy Warrior*. It was written by Henry Newbolt and was addressed to boys. The stories were of kings and knights and carnage and chivalry and heroic, glorious deaths. There were detailed and resplendent pictures of slaughtered heathen, wide-eyed and white-teethed, and French men-at-arms stuck with arrows writhing in agony before English bowmen. Instinctively she had known that her father would scorn the book, particularly its archaically expressed sentiments of affected honour and tradition, and that she must never show or mention it to anyone, not even her brother, for fear of confiscation. She never had, and the book was now hidden in a drawer under her underclothes. It still exerted a fascination that made her feel guilty and fearful and excited. She knew why; it was because its opinions were so foreign to her own upbringing and background. In Henry Newbolt's eyes a bookworm was as bad as a sneak, and a boy's greatest love should be fighting.

For a long time she had treated herself to the occasional chivalric daydream. In these flights of fancy, her faith was not always unambiguous, though she was invariably known as Jessica. Sometimes she was rescued at the last moment from the vilest depredations of the cruel infidel by a comely and chaste knight. At others, she herself would save a stalwart, warmongering crusader from sacrifice to his bloodthirsty Cross. And at night, when her dreams were spontaneous, there were not entirely taintless involvements with noblemen of iron, or romantically fated liaisons with dazzling pursuivants of the Holy Grail. Always, there was a shadowy figure, often draped with a cloak, whose face she was never able to see. Perhaps it was her guardian angel; perhaps it was her lord and master biding his time. Sometimes she awoke to a sense of shame.

Her faith was as much part of her and was as essential to her as her blood. The God of her Fathers was her God. How then could she even pretend that her husband-to-be was *nicht von unserer*? It was shocking and, when she wasn't pretending, made her hate herself. It was as if she were two people: one, the dutiful daughter who practised the ancestral faith and honoured her parents; the other, a deceitful shikse who dallied with sheygets and was so degraded that she could contemplate apostasy. Her father knew nothing of this but he must have feared it, for not long ago he had made her learn by heart a chilling caution:

'Every Jew who contemplates marriage outside the pale must regard himself as paving the way to a disruption which would be the final, as it would be the culminating, disaster in the history of his people.'

It was laughably unlikely that she would meet and fall in love with a Christian, but if that remote and undesired possibility occurred, there was a way. It had happened to an American friend of her cousin. On holiday in England, she had been introduced to and fallen for, of all people, a Norfolk pig-farmer. He had converted, and was now a highly respected and learned rabbi in Hartford, Connecticut. Orthodox, too.

She knew she was being silly, but that was what happened in the early hours. Night was fading; soon she would discover whether the Lord was still in the house. She sat up in bed. The trouble with being a woman was that you felt you existed only through others. Men were lucky; they felt others only existed through them. She arranged the shoulder-straps of her nightie and then crossed her arms. What was really extra-ordinary – much too odd to be merely coincidental – was that the only member of the nobility she had ever met should bear the same name as that most renowned of knights.

Chapter Twenty-Five

IT WAS his second meeting with the doctor since his humiliating collapse at the dining-table. He remembered little of what had happened at the first; it had taken place the following day when he was still in a state of shocked exhaustion, but there had been endless tests.

'So, Arthur, how do you feel?'

'Exhausted, permanently exhausted.'

'I'm not surprised. By the way, are you happy to be called Arthur still?'

'I suppose I'm gradually settling into it. Did you see my announcement in *The Times?*'

'I must have missed it. What do your family think?'

'It's caused universal consternation and been roundly condemned, which convinces me I made the right decision.'

'Names are funny things. I've often wondered if they don't partly condition us. A Morris Greenberg I once knew changed his name to Maurice Vermont and became totally a different person. Worse, actually.'

The doctor laughed, a sonorous laugh that shook his whole body. He was plumper, his moustache and hair glossier. Arthur had never seen him look so unaffectedly happy.

'I suppose you're dying to hear the results of the latest tests.'

'I wouldn't put it quite like that.'

'The pain in your back, how is it?'

'I told you last time, it's gone.'

'And it hasn't come back?'

'No.'

'Do you believe in miracles?'

'No.'

117

'As a doctor, I don't either. Instead we call it immuno-therapy.'

'That rings a bell.'

'It means the spontaneous regression of inoperable cancer. Do you understand what I'm saying?'

Dr Israel interlaced his chubby fingers and laid his arms on the desk. His smile was pure sweetness. Arthur felt more unworthy than the prodigal son.

'Arthur, I'm trying to tell you that, no thanks to me, you're in the clear. There is no trace of cancer left.'

'Why me?'

'My God, that's what people say when they're told they've got cancer.'

Neither Arthur's bearing nor his expression had changed since he had sat down. His legs were still crossed, his folded hands rested in his lap, and his lips were set in a wry smile that the doctor's daughter might have described as nobly disdainful.

'It's a bit difficult to take in. I mean it changes everything.'

'It certainly does; it is living instead of dying.'

'That's the difficulty, living is infinitely more troublesome. Things you probably take for granted – a home, an income, friends – I've got rid of them all.'

'You've had them before, you can have them again.'

'Yes, but I've changed. I've come to hate – no, not to hate, not even to despise – but to regret, and I suppose almost feel sorry for my old self. I thought ... oh hell, I'm treating you like a confessional.'

'Go on, I'm listening.'

'I said to myself, your life has been fatuous and futile, it'll be no loss to you or anybody else. Death will be an escape from all the messes and flops you've made of it. And now I haven't got that easy way out. I've got to start again, like a child learning everything from the beginning. I can't go back to the old ways. I don't even want to.'

'Would you like a drink?'

'No, I don't think so. What I'm trying to say is that the future is bloody frightening because I no longer know anything about myself except that I know what I don't like.'

'That's something. Perhaps you would like me to change your prognosis.'

They smiled at each other in an easy silence. Arthur saw the neat row of pebbles on the mantelshelf and wondered if he had changed at all and was not still the same egotist he claimed to have buried.

'I suppose I should say thank you.'

'Can I help at all?'

'You know it's up to me. There is one thing though, would you allow me to see your daughter?'

Hardly perceptibly Dr Israel shivered. That possibility had never occurred to him.

'Why on earth should you want to?'

'There's a goodness about her, an innocence. I need her inspiration.'

'Esther is very young you know, almost a child still.'

'But would you?'

'She knows so little of the ways of the world. I admit she has been brought up very sheltered.'

'I only want to learn from her as a friend.'

'What you ask is very hard for me because of the danger. I tell you, if that happened, in my eyes she would be as good as dead.'

'I don't understand. What danger?'

'If she fell in love with you and lost her faith. Our religion is more important to us than yours is to you. It is all we have. And Miriam and Esther are all I have left. But, having said that, I reluctantly give you permission.'

'I said just now that only I could help myself. It isn't true, you know that.'

And then to their mutual embarrassment Arthur burst into tears.

Chapter Twenty-Six

BRIAR rang Bel. She recognized his voice at once.
'Darling, how nice to hear from you again so soon.'
'I did enjoy tea with you the other day. Sumptuous.'
'It was lovely seeing you.'

'I wondered if I could come again some time. It was such fun gassing with you and I'd love to hear more about your beautiful pictures.'

'Of course, darling, any time. I'm glad you appreciate the paintings. I'm so happy that somebody in the family does at last. They *are* rather special.'

'How about Tuesday week?'

'Lovely. I'll expect you about four.'

Well pleased, Briar replaced the receiver. He looked with respect at the iron chisel he'd borrowed from a building site. He was certain he would suffer no compunction. After all, he was doing her a favour; opening up the gates of heaven.

Chapter Twenty-Seven

RESPONSES to the news of Arthur's cure varied among his family, friends and acquaintances. Rejoicing was by no means vocal or even universal, perhaps because of the traditional English wariness of the miraculous, perhaps because of a distaste for impetuous jubilation. But it was not altogether absent.

Bel went straight down on her knees and remained there for some hours, much to Francis's perplexity and irritation. She even remembered to offer up thanks for the prayers of the youth on the 137 bus.

At Lingfield Place, Reverend Mother Euberta broke the good news to the assembled Little Sisters of St Luke. She spoke of the cure as if it were the only possible outcome of their prayers. But in spite of her assured words, she was dumbfounded. She could only believe that Lord Lingfield had suffered from nothing worse than an undiagnosed bout of lumbago. However, the Little Sisters were visibly, if restrainedly, overjoyed, so at the end of her talk she allowed them to clap and promised them orange ice lollies for the following day.

Afterwards, in the privacy of her office, she prayed for guidance on how best to publicize and capitalize on this heavenly windfall. If that were the right expression.

Hermione, who heard the news in a roundabout way from Bobo, who'd heard it from Moyra, was quite pleased because she was fond of Bliss, though she couldn't imagine why he'd adopted such a boorish name and she had no intention of using it. The only other Arthur she'd ever known was her father's carpenter, a nice man but none the less working class. There was a fly in the ointment however, and that was that

121

she'd stupidly let the cat out of the bag. Believing that Bliss was on his way out, she had told her husband in a moment of post-coital tenderness of her foolish escapade with him. He had taken it like a man and caressingly forgiven her, and since then their marriage had been as active as never before. But when he discovered that his wife's lover was less dead than resurrected, she doubted whether he would be so magnanimous or so ardent. She was sure Bliss wouldn't be so rash as to renew his attentions. But if he did? The trouble was that she was like putty in his hands.

In the City, Simon was unconcerned about the pathological and thaumaturgical implications of Arthur's return from the grave's edge. His question was not how Arthur still came to be living, but how on earth he could afford to. He very much hoped that his one-time client would not have the gall to come to him for advice.

Such was the dowager Lady Lingfield's jubilation that she was almost able to forgive the appalling central European doctor for his apathy and professional incompetence. The core of her happiness, as she repeatedly reminded herself, was that her son, her flesh and blood, who was for dead, was now living and well. It was true there was another ground for rejoicing, but it was one she admitted only to herself and then only grudgingly. His survival removed a dark, horrid threat to her; that of being abandoned to self-reliance. She was not a proud woman, she knew her limitations; she accepted she could not cope without a strong man to fall back on. Such a man was the redeemed lion of her loins; he would defend her against the wiles of a widow-despising world, not to mention the idiosyncrasies of her demented brother. But there lay a fresh worry, for Clarry had changed. He appeared to be virtually normal. He was always properly dressed, or rather no longer assumed impromptu *déshabillé*. Gone were the idiotic word games and, though the counting continued, it was done in private and not broadcast. In a way the change was more provoking than the old dottiness because it suggested that Clarry was up to something, something probably very outlandish indeed.

Moyra was relieved, too. She had always disapproved of Arthur dying. She recognized that the death of a first, albeit ex, husband would age her in the eyes of her friends and encourage those who were less kindly disposed to put her down as positively senile. She was also aware that it was very much harder to pick holes in the dead than the living.

Crécy honoured the good news, with Rollo Saxmundham's aid, by accidentally conceiving. In addition, she sent her father a Cornish piskie good-luck charm. Surprised as he was at being given it, he deplored its rascally expression and, thinking it might be a jinx, he hid it in a drawer under his socks.

However, the most extreme responses came from Clarry and Briar. Lady Lingfield was right, Clarry had changed. The manic joviality had been replaced by a contented tranquillity. It was suggested by some that he'd been lobotomized. Not a trace of his buying mania remained, hardly even the recollection. There were a few quirks that lingered, but these he indulged in the privacy of his room. But the greatest change his sister was ignorant of, and it concerned his future. Through Bel, he had made arrangements to remove to Lingfield Place. It was his act of thanksgiving for his nephew's cure. In return for a boxlike room next to the potting-shed and three meals a day, he was to help in the garden and about the house. Reverend Mother had made two stipulations, which she disguised to Clarry as acts of obedience; he was to remain for ever silent unless addressed, and he was to continue counting for as long as he was able. He had bowed to both with a serene resignation that had made Reverend Mother wonder whether she was doing the right thing. Certainly Clarry was not the munificent repercussion of the miracle that she had hoped for.

The extremity of Briar's response was that he showed no response at all. He spoke to no one, met with no one; with patience he awaited his teatime date with Bel.

Chapter Twenty-Eight

BEL had put out her prettier tea-service. A Worcester set, each flimsy piece was decorated with wickerwork baskets of glorious fruit and rococo shields of royal blue. On the two chargers was a variety of extraordinarily thinly-cut sandwiches: cucumber and salmon, egg mayonnaise, potted lobster and, for old time's sake, mustard and cress. Just in case Briar still had a sweet tooth she had prepared a few strawberry jam sandwiches. The whole fruits bulged from the slices of bread. She surveyed the table with pride: she had surpassed herself.

It was only recently that she had discovered what a nice young man her great-nephew had turned into. She had not known him well as a child, but now, quite apart from his interest in the arts, she found him the most accessible and amusing of her family. She was flattered that he should have invited himself, particularly so soon after his last visit. On a side table stood two cakes; one almost black, oozing chocolate cream; the other plainer, festooned with plump raspberries.

She had brought out some books she thought might interest him and that might further kindle his enthusiasm for her paintings, for she had made up her mind. That very morning, she had appended yet another codicil to her will. She was undecided whether to tell him; on the whole she thought it better not to. The books were temptingly laid out on a sofa table: Raymond Lister's study of Edward Calvert, Lord David Cecil's biography of Samuel Palmer and a catalogue of the Ashmolean Museum.

Two pots of tea stood steaming on a hotplate: Lapsang Souchong and Earl Grey – it was pure extravagance but, as she so rarely entertained, she readily forgave herself. Francis

124

crouched on the sofa, eating a banana. He had already made off with a sandwich and she was anxious that he shouldn't attack the cakes with his nimble fingers.

Briar was just a little late. At times she worried if she might not be guilty of feeding off the young. Their vitality and exuberant imagination were enticing and, she hoped, contagious. Yet, she prided herself on never having been a lonely person. Although much of her adult life had been spent alone, she had never been needy. She felt she had the resourcefulness of those who are without superfluous resources. Francis was her only extravagance and it was true, she did worry about what would happen to him should anything happen to her. He would not be happy in a menagerie. She waited for footsteps outside her front door with undeniable delight. Expectantly she nibbled a vegetarian sandwich and listened.

Briar bludgeoned her with his borrowed chisel almost as soon as he came in. He hit her three times about the head and body before the screeching monkey intervened and caused confusion. He swung at the creature, which fell on the table of food. He struck out again and the pretty pieces of china flew into the air like bulldozed mosaics. Bel lay still in an armchair, as if she were catnapping. A small drop of blood trembled on her earlobe. The monkey cowered in a corner squealing. He hit it in the back of the neck and it collapsed and was silent. He removed the paintings from the walls and left. Steam still seeped from the spouts of the teapots.

Chapter Twenty-Nine

'IF YOU really want to know what makes orthodox Jews tick, you ought to read the Pentateuch and the Haftorahs with commentary.'

'The what?'

'It's the book they use in synagogues. It's in English as well as Hebrew.'

It was not what Simon said, but the way he said it that suggested that he thought Arthur's interest in Judaism was degenerate.

From Hermione's husband, who spoke several languages and was therefore considered a polymath by his friends, Arthur learnt that the likeliest place to find such a recondite book was in one of the few remaining second-hand bookshops in the Charing Cross Road. From several of the dealers there, he learnt that the only person who could possibly help him was Mr Mowinckel of Stamford Hill.

The Underground journey to Stamford Hill took half an hour, but Arthur had not walked far from the station before he realized that he had travelled much further. He had seen photographs of European ghettos of fifty, sixty years ago. Now he was in one and nothing but the prim, English suburban architecture was changed. He felt a stranger. The men he had passed in the streets were all bearded, tieless and uniformly dressed in black hats and long grey frock-coats. The earnest-faced children, sedately returning home from school, seemed to have sidestepped childhood. Especially the overdressed bespectacled boys with their beaver hats and coils of hair hanging from their temples. And why were all the women he saw primped and glossy-haired and why were they all pushing prams? It was hardly credible that the entire female population of Stamford Hill consisted of young Jewish mothers who all happened to wear wigs.

The sense that he had slipped out of time present was increased by his apparent invisibility. Nobody cast him so much as a glance. And yet in his pinstripe suit he must have appeared as strange to these people as they did to him. By the time he reached the door of Mr Mowinckel's terrace house, his feeling of separation was such that he doubted whether he should have been there at all. Nevertheless, he rang the bell.

'Shalom.'

The man who opened the door looked like a wasted and drab Father Christmas. He had a long white beard and wore the ubiquitous black hat and grey frock-coat. He bowed and ushered Arthur into the house. Books packed the hall and piles of them ascended the stairs. The ground-floor room that Arthur was led into was lined with books. There was a musty smell of dust and crumbling paper. The only furniture was a massive wooden table. This too was spread with books. Arthur felt panic creeping in. He was a pariah, a barbarian intruding into an elect and exclusive race. His clothes felt comically wrong, he might just as well have appeared naked and uncircumcised.

'I rang you.'

Mr Mowinckel bowed his head.

'Do you remember? It was concerning the Pentateuch.'

Mr Mowinckel bowed again. He was sparing with his words.

'Perhaps I should explain, I'm not Jewish. I don't know if it matters, I mean, as far as selling me the book.'

Mr Mowinckel waited.

'Actually, I'm Church of England, but non-practising to be honest. I should have told you on the telephone, I'm sorry.'

Almost imperceptibly, Mr Mowinckel shrugged his shoulders. He smiled sardonically.

'Why should I deny you the Sacred Text? It will be a jewel in your home.'

'To be frank, I can't claim to be a very religious man.'

Athur wanted to call the old man something but didn't know what. He inclined to Father, but it didn't sound quite right. He wished he'd done a little bit of Judaic homework.

127

' "Lift up thine eyes unto heaven." Did you know that astronomy and adoration entered the world together?'

'To tell the truth, I've never really thought about it.'

To be gone, preferably with the book, if necessary without it, was Arthur's sole wish. Standing around in a dusty, dim room listening to the philosophical intimacies of a crank from another world and age was unsettling.

'Are you uneasy? Don't be. It has been written that if a Jew attacks a Christian, a fellow Jew must go to the aid of the Christian. We are a people of love and peace.'

Arthur thought of the Middle East, but said nothing.

'I would like to buy the book, please.'

'Joseph ben Judah ibn Aknin said, "Make study of the Torah your chief interest in life; let all your other occupations be secondary to it." '

'How much is it?'

'Machsor Vitry said, "The Torah was given to man as a gift." '

Arthur was taken aback. Not having anticipated generosity, he was devoid of eloquent expressions of gratitude.

'Heavens! You can't do that, it's too much.'

'In one volume – ten pounds, or I have a set ... '

'Whichever is cheaper.'

'The one volume is ten pounds.'

'I'll take it.'

Arthur wondered whether Mr Mowinckel intended that he should feel like a lecher haggling with a father over the price of his untouched girl.

The dark blue book was produced and laid on the table.

'If you are paying by cheque, please put your address on the back. Whatever faith you hold, even if you have no faith at all, it would be wrong of you to put any other book on top of this. I'm sure you know.'

'Of course.'

Arthur couldn't believe that the old man didn't want to know why he was buying the book.

'Perhaps I should tell you why I want it?'

But having said that Arthur could think of no sensible reason. Because he was no longer dying of cancer. Because he was a student of liturgy. Because he envied the spiritual strength he suspected he'd found in a Jewish girl he'd met once and with whom he'd exchanged three sentences. Because her father was the only man he'd ever admired. None of them sounded credible. The serene stoicism of the old man was irritating.

'Have you lived here long?'

'Yes, thank you.'

Courteously, but unwaveringly, Arthur was led to the front door.

'Perhaps you are a righteous gentile in embryo.'

Mr Mowinckel smiled as he spoke and then bowed his head. 'Shalom.'

Arthur nodded back enthusiastically. He hadn't an idea what he was on about but the prospect of fresh air, time present and the familiarity of central London was refreshing. Clutching his prize he walked smartly back to the Underground station.

Arthur sat in the train and read randomly.

Finsbury Park.

'While recognizing the sacred nature of the estate of wedlock, Judaism prescribes continence even in marriage. "The Jewish ideal of holiness is not confined to the avoidance of the illicit; its ideal includes the hallowing of the licit." (Moore). It ordains the utmost consideration for the wife not only throughout the monthly period of separation (*niddah*), but also during the seven following days of convalescence and recovery (*taharah*), which are terminated by ritual purification through total immersion either in a fountain, or a "gathering of living water ..." '

Arsenal.

'Striking testimony has been given by scientists to the fact that, though health is not put forward as the primary purpose of these regulations, yet such is their indubitable result ... While medical opinion is not unanimous on this difficult subject, there can be no doubt as to the significance of statistics like the following: an investigation, conducted over a number of years at Mount Sinai Hospital, New York, in connection with eighty thousand Jewish women who observe ... '

Holloway Road.

'... *niddah* and *taharah* laws, showed that the proportion of those suffering from uterine cancer was one to fifteen of non-

129

Jewish women of corresponding social and economic status.'

Trust the Jews to be so thorough, thought Arthur.

Caledonian Road.

'A red heifer, free from blemish and one that had not yet been broken to the yoke, was to be slain outside the camp. It was then to be burned, cedar-wood, hyssop, and scarlet being cast upon the pyre. The gathered ashes dissolved in fresh water, were to be sprinkled on those who had become contaminated through contact with a dead body.

'This ordinance is the most mysterious rite in Scripture, the strange features of which are duly enumerated by the Rabbis. Thus, its aim was to purify the defiled, and yet it defiled all those who were in any way connected with the preparation of the ashes and water of purification. "It purifies the impure, and at the same time renders impure the pure!" So inscrutable was its nature – they said – that even King Solomon in his wisdom despaired of learning the secret meaning of the Red Heifer regulations.'

'..."A virgin shall conceive." Christian scholars today admit that "virgin" is a mistranslation for the Hebrew word *almah* ...'

King's Cross.

Bemused and interested as he was by the fat book, he hid it in an abandoned plastic shopping-bag. It wasn't that he was anti-Semitic, but he feared that the bold, gold Hebraic characters stamped on the book would mark him out as different now that he was back in the real world.

Chapter Thirty

THEY met outside her father's hospital at precisely two. Arthur had considered asking her to lunch but had changed his mind because he didn't want her family – actually her father – to have the slightest grounds for thinking him presumptuous. The hospital forecourt, familiar to them both, commended itself as a suitably neutral and innocent rendezvous.

Esther was even smaller than he'd remembered her. She wore a yellow frock with leg-of-mutton sleeves. It was patterned with red sailing boats. Worn by a pretty girl with a penchant for nostalgia it might have looked stylish; on Esther it merely looked dowdy. They shook hands; hers were tiny and damp. She was clearly ill at ease. He wondered why she had agreed to come. Perhaps, paradoxically, her father had insisted that she should.

'So kind of your father to allow you to accompany me.'

'He asked me whether I wanted to, you know.'

She smiled, but the gentle reproof was there.

'And, of course, extremely decent of you. I hope you won't be too bored.'

'I am hardly ever bored.'

They went by train from Victoria. On the telephone Arthur had emphasized that they would have to travel by public transport. Several times he had asked her whether she would mind the discomfort. She had wondered then, and still did, whether he was trying to dissuade her from coming. The occasion of the outing, to visit Arthur's old nanny, was odd too. She could well understand why he should wish to see her; she could not understand why he should want a virtual stranger to accompany him. Not that she really regarded herself as that.

The shabby train wound through the drab land of south London. Outside the bleary windows were rows of brick terraces and stunted concrete high-rises. Esther and Arthur faced each other; there was no one else in the compartment.

'I'm told it's become almost fashionable to live here.'

'Yes?'

Before she had rather dreaded being alone with him; now she felt unfearful. He was nothing like the man she had imagined on the night of his collapse. His resignation and detachment, if neither exactly knightly nor courtly, were qualities she was unaccustomed to and, if only because of them, he interested her. Possibly she was deluding herself, but she believed that instinctively she discerned him.

'When did you last see your nanny?'

'More than twenty years ago, I'm afraid.'

The train paused by an immense advertising hoarding that showed a stretched bed full of laughing men and women of every race and colour. A Mountie lay beside a geisha who lay beside a sheikh who lay ... Esther wondered whether it promoted miscegenation or merely racial harmony.

'Are you sure she's still alive?'

'Who?'

'Your nanny.'

'Oh, yes, she regularly sends me a present on my birthday and at Christmas.'

'If you think I'm prying, just tell me to mind my own business, but why are you seeing her after all this time?'

'When I was ill, I promised myself I would. And guilt, mostly guilt.'

The train lurched forward. She didn't know how to phrase her next question. Perhaps as straightforwardly as possible; after all he didn't seem to resent her curiosity.

'Why did you want me to come with you? I'm glad you did, but ... '

'I couldn't think of anybody else who would.'

It was as bad as she'd feared. Serve her right for being so nosy.

They were the only people to get off the train. They left the station behind them and walked down a broad, tree-lined

132

avenue. It was deathly quiet; they might have been trespassers on a deserted film set. No sight or sound of traffic, no human movement, the trees hardly stirred.

'Do you know where to go?'

'I looked it up on a map.'

The semi-detached houses though essentially similar were all superficially different. A bow-window added here, a portico there, a minute conservatory – all bore witness to the irrepressible urge of man for self-expression.

'Will she recognize you, does she know we're coming?'

'It's an act of, I hope, divine impulse. By the way, I meant to tell you, I've bought a copy of your holy book.'

There wasn't time for a response; they had stopped outside a pebble-dashed house painted a vivid gorse colour.

'I think this is it.'

'It's just an ordinary house.'

'It's the right number.'

By the door was a rustic wooden plaque with the etched name 'Havenhome'. Arthur rang the bell. The upper part of the front door was made of mottled glass. For a long time nothing quivered in it but then there were shifting flecks of colour, blue and flesh and grey, and at last a pale, gaunt-faced woman in a shiny nylon quasi-uniform opened the door.

'We're closed. They're all bedded down.'

'We've come a long way to see my old nanny, Miss Hooper.'

The woman had specks of egg-yolk in the corners of her mouth. She held the door against them half-resolutely.

'What's the name?'

'Lord Lingfield.'

'Come in.'

The hallway was a short, narrow passage carpeted with a pattern of cream fleurs-de-lis on a gold background. On the mock-pine-papered walls were lurid photographs of faraway lakes and snow-capped mountains. Two half-opened doors and a flight of stairs led away from the hallway. The quasi-uniformed woman led them to the bottom of the stairs. The aroma of overcooked cabbage was so strong it should have been tangible.

'It was Miss Hooper you wanted to see?'

'That's right.'

Through one of the half-open doors Esther spied three men sleeping on closely-packed camp beds. It was still quite early in the afternoon. An unpleasant, sweetish smell came from the room and mingled with that of the cabbage.

'Miss Hooper is no longer here.'

'Are you sure? I had a card from her only recently.'

The names of the men were written above their beds: Joe, Leslie, Peter. Their clothes, neatly folded, lay on bedside chairs.

'Miss Hooper has gone on.'

'Where to?'

Through the second half-open door more cramped beds were visible. There was an occasional, meaningless sigh, like the moan of a sleeping dog in the night.

'Miss Hooper passed over some weeks ago. I can give you the date, if you don't mind waiting.'

They walked back to the station. Arthur held Esther's arm. She was undecided whether it was for support or out of remorse or amorousness.

'I'm sorry to have wasted your time.'

She didn't believe he had. She suspected he hadn't the slightest idea of what it must have been like for his nanny to have been stuck in such a house – she couldn't bring herself to call it a home – for over twenty years. Continually to be bereft of any privacy and to be faced with the animal nature of other abandoned humans for all those years must have been more terrible than the longest prison sentence. Probably her only contact with the outside world was her callous, former charge whose vapid existence she loyally acknowledged to the last with her bi-annual presents. For what in return? Dereliction and two dull, dutiful thank-you letters a year. Oh yes, she had been fed, kept warm and clothed, but for what possible purpose? Esther walked apart from Arthur.

'I was wondering if you'd care to come back for a bite to eat?'

The bosky avenues were as empty as before. Only an untended milk-float suggested the possibility of human activity.

'I couldn't. I must go home.'

'I've prepared a small supper. I asked your father. He said it was permissible.'

The quaint, late-Victorian, red-brick station was in sight. For Esther it might have been touched by the Shekinah, it was the glorious gateway to home and love and integrity. She hardly heard Arthur.

'I want to thank you for coming. I didn't know she wouldn't be there. I didn't know she'd died. I think you'll find the meal is kosher.'

She smiled, in spite of herself.

'It can't be. What is it?'

'Pâté, steak and ice-cream. I told you, I've been reading the Chumash.'

She laughed.

'You'll have to eat it all yourself. It certainly isn't kosher.'

They were on the deserted platform and a train was pulling in. It was an absurd fancy and it only lasted a second but Arthur imagined that he was pushing her in front of the train. It was to punish her for her infallibility, for excluding him from her world.

'We'll travel back together?'

'It's wonderful we understand each other. My father will be relieved.'

They both laughed.

Esther sat in the black armchair in Arthur's small flat.

'I really can't eat any of it.'

The dish of pork pâté and the slab of mauve steak lay on top of the diminutive refrigerator.

'I can't stay more than half an hour, my parents will be worried.'

Arthur hovered by the scant bottles in the kitchenette.

'I need to get extremely drunk, otherwise I won't be able to tell you.'

'Do you have any tea?'

'You realize you're young enough to be my daughter?'

'Earl Grey, if you have it, with a slice of lemon, please.'

Arthur switched on the kettle and poured himself a large measure of whisky. Drink was supposed to obliterate inhibition; he would only know what he wanted to tell her and only be able to express it when he lacked restraint. He swallowed the drink in a gulp.

'What do you want to tell me?'

For someone who was less than half his age her pointedness was inspiring. He poured himself another jigger.

'Esther, I think lurking deep down in every Englishman there's a trace of anti-Semitism.'

'Why are you telling me?'

He made the tea and fumbled about in the refrigerator.

'I'm sorry, there's no lemon.'

'I don't think I've ever seen anybody drunk before, except in the films. My father says it's not something Jews do much.'

'I'm afraid I'm going to disappoint you, I don't think I can.'

'I still don't see why you want to.'

'I wish I'd had a child as sane as you. I want to be able to put what I feel into words.'

'That you hate me and my race?'

'No, it's more complicated than that. I suppose I'm envious of you, of your family, and your people. You're such a superior élite. I suppose I do hate your exclusivity, but only because I would like to be included.'

It was only part, and the smaller part, of what he wanted to say. He wanted to tell this plain, unfashionable girl that for some unfathomable reason he depended on her companionship and feared that she might remove it. He didn't know how to.

'I'm sometimes jealous of gentiles, their sophistication, their freedom.'

'Oh that! You have only to look at my children to see what that's worth.'

'I'd forgotten that you're married.'

'Was.'

He looked away. It could have been out of grief or embarrassment or boredom. She wished he'd leave the kitchenette and come and sit down.

'Esther, I think your father is the most impressive man I've ever met.'

'So do I, but, of course, I haven't met many.'

Arthur poured himself another drink; with theatrical deliberation he moved into the living area. Perhaps he was proving himself wrong.

'You've heard of Abelard and Heloïse, and Dante and Beatrice?'

136

'Of course.'

'I'm mad. I don't even mean what I'm saying, but just think what the fruit of the union between a Jewish girl and an Englishman would be.'

'If I know what you're thinking, my family would disown me. Is there more tea?'

He overlooked her question and tugged at an ear lobe. He was talking nonsense but he was verging on what he wanted to say. He just needed time.

'Why did you buy the Chumash?'

'To learn.'

'Did you?'

'Only the gulf.'

She spoke his name for the first time. It sounded contrived.

'Arthur, if we had a child would it be Jewish or gentile?'

'I simply don't know. It's what I'm trying to tell you. I probably wouldn't be brave enough.'

'Brave enough?'

He sat down on the sofa, there was only room for two. Their knees touched inadvertently. Her freckles, her propinquity, her ingenuousness – perhaps it was his whisky, but he felt, if not an attraction, a certain degree of warmth.

'If I'd been at Treblinka and I was told to, I would probably have pushed you and our baby in.'

He remembered at school the gush of pleasure cruelty gave. She said nothing.

'There's this frightful, terrible dichotomy inside me.'

'Do I only interest you because of what I am, not who I am?'

'I merely hope I would have had the courage to wear the yellow star in Prague or Paris or wherever.'

'I thought that was history. You've reminded me that it isn't.'

He spluttered, some of his drink ran down his chin.

'You didn't know me before, I was a much worse person. I honestly think being with you makes me better. You're a transforming angel. By the way, do Jews have angels?'

'I only really respect people who practise their religion, whatever it is.'

'Has anybody told you you're a stuck-up prig?'

She felt self-consciously old, as if she were ageing years in seconds.

'I must go home now. My parents will be worried.'

'I'm sorry, I'll take you home. I didn't explain what I meant very well. It's just that not having Judaism, I feel deprived. But please never tell anyone that.'

Esther stood up. She had an unpleasant foreboding that Arthur was about to make a horrid fool of himself or to plunge her into a great sadness.

'I'll be all right by myself in a taxi. You've helped me grow up a lot, thank you.'

'Oh, Christ, you still don't understand. I need to share your people's suffering.'

'My father will be getting concerned.'

'God's such a shit not to let you love me.'

'Please ring for a taxi. You don't need to come with me.'

He was leaning forward on the sofa, away from her. His resignation was suggested in the line of his shoulders and his dishevelled hair.

'One last thing. Will you come with me to Tilbury?'

'Tilbury? Why Tilbury?'

'Because I need you to be with me.'

Chapter Thirty-One

BRIAR was haggard. For three days and nights, he had stayed in his room. He slept in spells that left him confused as to the time and more exhausted than before. Of the food he had been brought he had been able to swallow little and that he had either vomited or scoured. The gentlest, unexpected sound was like a siren screaming in his head. He lived in fear. Fear that he would be detected. Fear that he would not. Fear that he would give himself up. Fear that he had lost his mind.

The silence was excruciating. There had been no report of Bel anywhere. Not in the papers, not on the television or radio, not even from the family. Sometimes he woke to the hope that he had dreamt the whole nightmarish event, but he had only to look at the small stack of paintings leaning against the wainscot to remind himself of the truth. The urge to make an anonymous telephone call to precipitate matters was almost irresistible, but he knew that it would be fatal as well as he knew it was only a question of time before he could resist no longer. The need to tell someone, anyone, what had happened was as potent as thirst. Once spoken of, the experience would be shared and some of the guilt relinquished.

He lay on his bed. Images that he could neither control nor dismiss barged before him like a parade of demonic clowns. Always there was the capuchin. Doubled up by pain, screeching and whimpering, baring its teeth in futile self-defence. Other monkeys dressed up as tinpot soldiers vaulted and whirled sickeningly past him. Bel was Christlike, meekly suffering the blows, offering nothing in return but the sorrowful look in her eyes. As if she were asking, 'Why are you doing this? It pains me because it will pain you.' And Travers,

Travers carefully distanced from the mêlée, his face beaming beneath a judge's wig, silkily reassuring Briar that he would never suffer the slightest remorse.

It was as involuntary as parturition: Briar sat on the edge of the bed and dialled Travers' number.

'I must see you.'

'How about lunch tomorrow?'

'No, now.'

'I'm sorry, I've got someone with me.'

'It has to be now.'

'What's the hurry?'

'I did what you told me to do.'

'I don't know what you're talking about.'

'I have the paintings. They're all yours. I never want to see them again.'

'You're making no sense. I'll ring you back when I'm free.'

'I'm on my way.'

Briar replaced the receiver. He had glimpsed light at the end of the tunnel and even if it wasn't daylight but the blaze of advancing nemesis that was preferable to the engulfing darkness.

Chapter Thirty-Two

GWYNN and Travers were separated by a low table; on it stood an ice-bucket and a bottle of pink champagne. Remembering the relish with which Travers had consumed a cocktail cherry, Gwynn was not vastly surprised by this choice of celebratory drink. Travers wiped an invisible line of foam from his upper lip and continued.

'You and I know they are brilliant, but the philistinism and parsimony of the super-rich is past belief. I can tell you now that I really had to labour for you.'

As he spoke he tapped a forefinger on a sheet of paper covered with figures.

'To be frank, it cost me plenty but I'm sure you will not be disappointed with your share. I've always maintained that genius should be properly rewarded and if I've made little or nothing at least I have the satisfaction of knowing that you have been handsomely treated.'

Travers swivelled the paper round so that Gwynn could see what he was talking about.

'I think originally I said I could get you between ten and twenty thou a picture. Well, I wasn't far out. With expenses deducted I managed to get you nine for each. So that's eighteen.'

Travers' index finger jabbed at the figures on the sheet.

'Less my ten per cent commission, that's eighteen hundred. That comes to sixteen thousand, two hundred. Less the two thousand pound advance. So that's fourteen thousand, two hundred, for which happy sum I have here a cheque payable to you. You'll be off to Tuscany soon I suppose?'

His grin was fulsome. He dangled the cheque between two fingers like a tart with a key to instant happiness.

'Exactly how much did you sell them for?'

Travers was so taken aback by the bluntness of the question that he tottered on the edge of telling him the truth. Only a flood of self-interest saved him.

'More champagne?'

'Travers, I want to know exactly what you got for them.'

But now it was too late for revelation; Travers was master of himself again.

'My dear Gwynn, to be honest, it wouldn't mean anything if I told you, I don't even know myself precisely. You see there are so many deductions to be made: pay-offs, travelling expenses – the number of times I had to fly to New York – hush-money, entertaining, research. And, sadly, interest in Derain and Matisse is not what it was.'

Gwynn's glass of champagne was untouched.

'What about the drawings?'

'I had to throw them in to effect the sale.'

'You realize if I come clean you'll fall with me.'

'On the contrary, I bought them in good faith. But for Heaven's sake, don't let's bicker, if you feel hard done by, and you really haven't any grounds to, I'll forsake my commission. It'll mean I'm out of pocket, but anything to keep you happy.'

'I don't want to rob you, but – '

'Well, that's that then. Let's drink to it. Much better to settle amicably, after all, I hope we'll do business again.'

The doorbell rang. Travers slipped the cheque back in his pocket. Gwynn looked apprehensive.

'Who on earth's that?'

'Probably that stupid boy Briar. I told him I couldn't see him.'

Gwynn was in a quandary, he had never met Briar and because he was Crécy's brother he had no wish to. On the other hand, Travers still had the cheque and he didn't want to leave without it. Reluctantly he decided that he had no option but to stay.

'I don't know if you two have met. Gwynn, this is Briar Lingfield. By the way, Briar, you look ghastly. What have you been up to?'

It was undeniable. His face was blotched and shrunken and

142

his black hair drooped in greasy straggles. His clothes looked slept-in. As he moved into the room a sickly smell billowed in his wake. He paid no attention to Gwynn but stood within a foot of Travers. He dropped a canvas grip on the sofa in front of him.

'They're for you, I never want to see any of them again. I can't stand it any longer and it's all thanks to you.'

The grip remained on the sofa. Gwynn noticed that standing as they were they formed an isosceles triangle.

'Oh, Briar, don't be so melodramatic. Sit down and have a drink. Look, pink champagne, your favourite.'

'No. I'll be going along now. They're all yours.'

Briar made no move to leave. Without enthusiasm Travers peered into the bag. He removed the contents: nine framed pictures. He sat down.

'My God, they're divine!'

He placed the paintings on the low table, changed the position of one, peered into another. He was in raptures. He spoke softly as if otherwise they might evanesce.

'Gwynn! Come quickly, look aren't they marvellous. Look at that moon.'

With bad grace, Gwynn approached. He wanted Briar to go. He wanted to get his cheque from Travers and, if possible, squeeze another one out of him for the forsaken commission. He leant over the sofa, over Travers' shoulder and cast a cursory glance at just one of the pictures. When he spoke, it was with the quiet authority of somebody who already knew most of the answer.

'Briar, where did you get these?'

Briar said nothing. It was Travers who answered, rather petulantly.

'It's none of your business, Gwynn. Why don't you go?'

'Oh, but it is.'

'What do you mean?'

'Exactly that, that it is my business. Or if you insist on my being scrupulous, that it once was. Though, of course, in those days I didn't get paid anything like so well as now.'

Travers looked from one to the other. He flapped his arms like a deranged hen as he spoke.

'Briar is this true?'

143

Briar said nothing. This time it was Gwynn who answered.
'How should he know?'

Briar, who had finally taken advantage of the invitation to sit down, put his head on his knees and mumbled incomprehensibly.

Travers rose from the sofa, sat down again, and rose once more. As he went to Briar, he glanced back at Gwynn, but Gwynn couldn't even affect a leer. He laid his hands gently on Briar's shoulders.

'How did you get these, darling?'

Briar replied without lifting his head.

'The way you told me to.'

'But it was only a joke.'

It was a roaring whisper. Travers shook him as he spoke again.

'Christ, darling! And all for nothing.'

Chapter Thirty-Three

THE ward was on the top floor of the hospital. It was a bright, cheerful room painted light apple-green. The dozen or so beds were placed around three walls and faced inwards. In the middle of the room was a large wooden table at which the less indisposed sat in the day and took their meals. On top of the bedside cupboards were bowls of fruit, cards and vases of flowers. Those most recently admitted had the most abundant displays.

It was time for visiting. Relatives and friends sat dumbstruck by their loved ones, desperate to know when they could decently leave. A raucous man pressed magazines on a woman whose sight had all but left her before swiftly leaving himself. Arthur sat by Bel.

She was propped up in bed with pillows, her hands lying on either side of her thighs. Her face was almost without expression, occasionally an eyelid flickered. Arthur held one of her hands and from time to time squeezed it. Quite apart from her wounds – the bruises on her face and the bald patches on her head where the stitches had been sewn – she had aged terribly. Her eyes had the distant gaze of the blind.

'Doctor will be along presently.'

The nurse retreated, quickly, before she could be questioned.

The fruit in Bel's bowl, untried by her, was rotting and patchy brown. It was hard to tell where the sweet smell of decomposition came from. The hothouse flowers were wilting. Someone approached. But it wasn't the doctor, it was Briar. He looked nervous, but then the young were never easy in the face of the old and dying.

'I'm very pleased to see you, Briar. It's good of you to have come.'

'How is she, Dad? Somehow I had to come.'

'I really don't know, I'm still waiting for the doctor. The nurse simply said that Bel was unaware.'

Briar skirted round the bed, perhaps to avoid Bel's implacable stare, and planted an apathetic kiss on her brow. Arthur wondered if there wasn't a responsive quiver in her eyebrows, but was sure he was mistaken.

'Can I help at all?'

The doctor was gangly and affable. He looked even younger than the proverbial policeman. Arthur withdrew a pace or two from Bel's bed, as if he doubted her condition and feared she might overhear him.

'I am Miss Lingfield's nephew. How is she?'

'You could say she is jolly lucky to be alive. She was cataleptic when she was brought in. Who found her?'

'Her neighbour. The police said she'd probably been lying there for three days.'

'Poor old thing. Are you next of kin?'

'I suppose so. Has she any chance of recovery?'

'From the surface wounds, absolutely yes. As for her mind ... '

Briar sat on the chair by her bed: a pair of stockings and a cardigan were draped over the back. She was inscrutable. He wondered how much she remembered. He said nothing, but smiled at her fixedly. His fear was as insistent and intense as that he had suffered when a boy of eleven. For a whole summer holidays he did not know for certain whether he had been observed at school *in flagrante delicto*. He wanted her to be dead and if not that incurable.

'Her vision is certainly impaired and she's incapable of speech. It's hard to ascertain whether she can understand what is said to her, because she has no means of responding. Unfortunately it's virtually impossible to tell whether the trauma is temporary or permanent. Time alone will tell.'

'Do you think she's able to recognize her family?'

'There's the tragedy. It's quite possible that though she is utterly incapable of communication her memory and intellect are intact.'

Briar spoke to the doctor for the first time. He fingered and peered at a corner of the bedside cupboard as he spoke.

146

'So that if her attacker was paraded before her she might recognize him, but be completely unable to let anyone know?'

'Precisely. It must be jolly frustrating for her, poor dear. If her intelligence is unaffected, there must be hundreds of things she's bursting to tell you both.'

Bel dimly watched her nephew and great-nephew departing. Each of them had kissed her demurely on the cheek, a peck, a sort of stage kiss, empty of meaning, that would have been suitable as a mark of respect given to a dead colleague. Not as significant as a Judas kiss; more the sort of kiss that Malenkov planted on Stalin as he lay on his bier.

She felt completely drained, not in her body, because that was a battered, defeated old thing, but in her mind and her heart. She couldn't imagine – and over and over again she had tried to – what devil had driven Briar. Just now, she had seen the unassuageable terror in the boy's face and she knew it would clutch him all his days.

She remembered bits. She remembered Francis's pitiful crying and her inept anger at the wholly needless destruction of her china. She remembered Briar wrenching her pictures from the walls. (It was droll that she had been so concerned that none of the family took any interest in them.) Then it was night, seemingly for weeks, and the greatest anguish had been thirst, a thirst that robbed her of all other sensations of pain. To alleviate this burning obsession she had thought of the Son of Man thirsting on the Cross and offered up her brief discomfort in thanks for His timeless Passion. And then, there was her neighbour, Miss Pennyfeather, standing in the doorway asking her why she hadn't brought her milk in.

If she were granted the enunciation of one question – and she knew that though she might be granted thousands, she would not be granted one – it would be to ask about Francis. She supposed he must be dead, but for a long time stricken in that room, she had heard moans and birdlike screeches. Perhaps they had been echoes of his torture reverberating in her head, or perhaps she had merely heard herself.

She knew nothing of medicine, but she doubted that she would ever be more than an intelligent cabbage and, ironically, in the eyes of the rest of the world, simply a cabbage. She

147

would lie motionless for months, maybe even years, visited less and less by everyone but Briar who, tortured by the possibility of her recovery, would come regularly to ensure that his secret and hers remained just that. His haunted face would haunt her and she would never be able to relieve or exorcize him of his torment. He could never know that though she could neither forget nor understand, she had forgiven him.

Chapter Thirty-Four

THE wind howled. Swirling clouds fled: a recession of snow angels.

'I don't really know how to explain it, not in words.'

The train, even more down at heel than the one they had travelled in on their fruitless visit to Nanny, ambled noisily through east London at rooftop level. There was no corridor. Esther, whose occasional flashes of recondite knowledge startled Arthur, fancied they were sealed in their compartment and jokingly alluded to Lenin and the Finland Station. The banquette seats had been resolutely slashed and only a little less roughly repaired. Graffiti were daubed on the walls in a medium that appeared to be unmentionable. Arthur, who sat across from Esther, stared at the grimy floor and stroked his moustache as if he were on the brink of discovering something. An abandoned local newspaper bore the headline 'M25 Shoreham Link Gets Go Ahead.' He was glad Bel would probably never know. To lose the paintings and the valley was more than anybody could bear in one lifetime.

'You know my father said this must be the last time?'

'Yes, he told me. He said my psychotherapy was over.'

'Why don't you challenge him to a duel?'

'We might hurt each other.'

'Will you miss me?'

She was guileless and childish. He wished she was his little sister, or daughter. He would have cherished her, shown her the ropes, pointed out the pitfalls. Even taught her some dress sense.

'Why couldn't we have gone somewhere prettier? I mean Hampton Court or Windsor and your old school, I've never been there?'

'Sorry, it has to be Tilbury. I can't tell you why, not so you'd understand. Perhaps something to do with completing a circle.'

'The wheel of life?'

'Oh, I don't think it's as serious as that.'

'Was I the only person who would come with you?'

The reproach was so slight he only just caught it. He looked up at her. He had hardly bothered to look at her until now. She was in white, a cotton frock with a full skirt; it was quite becoming.

'Don't be so silly!'

'Did you live in Tilbury?'

'Of course not. I told you, I went there as a child to say goodbye to someone going to Australia. I knew Australia was far away, so I assumed Tilbury must be the beginning of the end of the world.'

The train halted. By the station stood a handsome red brick eighteenth-century house, beside it an ancient stone church and beyond a bulgy-walled pub. The trio faced a battery of oil storage tanks, feeder pipes and processors around which cows incongruously grazed.

'You never told me before. I think you have a death wish, like Keats, or was it Shelley?'

She spoke in questions; it was funny it hadn't occurred to him before.

'When I was in hospital I promised myself I'd come, just as I did with Nanny.'

She thought of making a joke about Tilbury, about hoping that it hadn't departed like Nanny, toppled off the edge of the world, but it would have been gratuitously cruel.

'You didn't even know me then.'

'That's true. I hardly know you now.'

The train jolted forward. The flat, treeless land ran down to the broad, featureless river. On the other side was more bleak land. He was comforted by her presence. He knew he still needed her for something, but he was no nearer to knowing what.

'How far is it, are we nearly there?'

Perhaps it was the love that his children had never given him; hers was such a child's question. They had betrayed him, he had betrayed them. But who first?

150

'Yes, nearly there.'

Once in Cyprus he had been playing poker in a bar, when some sharp young Parisian Jews on their way to a kibbutz had joined the game. Several hours later, humbled and out of pocket, he had gone outside and sat at a table overlooking the sea. A Jewish girl was sitting there, almost invisible in the dark. She was going back to England from Israel. She had bemoaned Israel, she hated its irreligion, its intolerance, its arrogant self-righteousness. He never knew her name and saw that she was plain, but for a long time afterwards he had thought of her. She too had prompted an indefinable need in him. Esther reminded him of her. The same beak. Perhaps it was as simple as that; perhaps that was all there was to it.

'Why do you want me to be with you sometimes? I don't understand.'

'Nor do I.'

'Are you lonely? The Talmud says that a man who is not married is not a complete man. Not that I'm suggesting.'

It saddened him that he knew she wasn't.

'You think too much.'

'It's a Jewish trait.'

The splendour of Tilbury Dockside Station was skeletal. Once the gateway to the ends of the earth, to grand ocean liners, the glamorous escape-hatch from grim mundanity, it was now the absurdly grandiose terminus of a shabby, short suburban line.

They stood outside the station wondering which uninviting way to go. A wicked, lazy wind blowing from the estuary cut through their skin and clothes to their bones.

'Now we're here, can we see some ships?'

There was nothing in the mud-coloured river but yellow froth and wooden spars and plastic drums. Arthur was glad he hadn't decided to end his days in its purging waters. He would merely have floundered in syrupy silt. They turned away from the river to the town.

'Oh, I would like to see some ships.'

He wondered how it had ever crossed his mind to kill her. But in reality he knew why; it was to deprive her father as he was depriving him.

'There's a policeman, we'll ask him.'

151

Dwarfed by high walls he stood guard in front of a great metal barrier, half a dozen notices repeated the message that there was no access without authority.

'Ships? Well, I might say you'd be better off in a museum. There aren't many now and those there are you can't see. To be truthful the few in here I wouldn't want to cross to Gravesend in.'

There was a pervasive, queasy reek of fuel oil and sulphur. Smoke and steam rose in lethargic billows from factory chimneys, hundreds of feet high.

'Tilbury's nothing much now, there's nothing to see. You from abroad?'

'London.'

'I knew you were tourists. Now you're here you could see the old fort. Elizabethan, so they say, and there's a smugglers' pub on the way.'

Following the policeman's directions they walked down a road of single-storey shops: a tattoo bar, a dress shop, whose window display suggested an earlier, more ingenuous age, and a quantity of taxi booths. These last in their profusion hinting that the people of Tilbury were not entirely blind to the delights of the outside world. The road came to an abrupt end. Beyond, towards the estuary, lay a wasteland of abandoned plots and contaminated streams, both gorged with indestructible rubbish. Three paint-blistered, quaintly twee bungalows lay low in this no man's land. All bore plaques on their doors indicating that they were concerned with man's salvation. 'Christian Witnesses for Pakistani and Indian Seaman', 'Mission to Jews, Turks and Infidels', 'The Acushla Church'. All three doors were secured with massive padlocks.

'What does Acushla mean?'

'You're Jewish, don't ask me. But it's a pity my Uncle Clarry isn't here, he'd doubtless know.'

The pockmarked road, once asphalted, had given way to ochre mud and stone. In waterlogged fields shaggy, stunted horses, mules and donkeys huddled together for protection from the brutal, blinding cold that pounded from the east. They shared the fields with sheets of rusting corrugated iron and plastic sacks that blew about in the wind like tumbleweed. Arthur and Esther turned the corner of a bank and ahead of

152

them at the end of the road a sagging clapboard inn crouched in a hollow.

'Good God, Esther, do you see what it's called? "The World's End".'

'I'm cold.'

'But don't you see what an incredible coincidence it is?'

'Yes.'

Esther hated Tilbury. Its horrid desolation reminded her of Malhausen. Her father had taken her there to show her what it meant to be Jewish. It was the first time she had understood. She hadn't realized before that she was different.

'Would you like a drink? It might be warm inside.'

'I feel out of place in pubs.'

They passed by and walked on towards the estuary. She raised her voice against the stealing wind and chanted.

> Ithaka gave you the splendid journey.
> Without her, you would not have set out.
> She hasn't anything else to give you.

'Who's Ithaka? What do you mean?'

'It's Cavafy, they're the only lines I can remember. It's why you wanted to come to Tilbury.'

'I still don't understand what you're talking about.'

'I think you do.'

She squeezed his arm once with a gloved hand. A flurry of icy rain swept over them. Minute spikes of drilling chill.

Tilbury's sour dereliction affronted her belief in the innate goodness of the world that God had created. It seemed to say that purposeless destruction, waste and ugliness were intrinsically part of life, were equal heirs of creation – even, perhaps, that corruption and mutilation would triumph in the end. Man was not Midas and everything he touched turned not to gold but to rubble and poisonous filth.

In the middle of a small patch of soggy marsh stood a diminutive fun-fair. There were just three booths, they huddled together, back to back, apparently defying both the ravaging weather and public indifference. From a tannoy fixed half-way up a central pole came scratchy, outdated pop music. At the top of the pole a tiny frayed pennant streamed. A handful of contemptuous children stood at a distance surveying the abject jollity.

Esther tugged Arthur's arm.

'Let's have a closer look.'

'I can't stand fiascos like that, they embarrass me.'

'At least it's trying to be cheerful and there's hardly anybody about.'

One of the booths was a carousel for toddlers; there were half a dozen brightly painted animals, a fire-engine with a brass bell and a miniature double-decker bus. A lanky and disreputable-looking man lounged against an emerald green duck. Next door was 'The Great Swan Dip'. A dozen plastic swans floated uncertainly in a bowl of water. The prizes: turquoise, mauve and orange-suited pierrette dolls were propped up in heaps at the back. A wrinkled and pasty-faced old woman, swathed in pieces of canvas, grinned and beckoned to them. To Arthur's shame, Esther behaved like a puppy on a leash. Her enthusiasm was incomprehensible.

'Can we have a go?'

'Must we? I find it utterly depressing.'

'Just to give the owners happiness.'

'Supposing you won one of those hideous dolls.'

'Well, let's see what's round the other side.'

The last booth was a shooting-gallery, pinned to a board at the back were a score of tattered playing-cards. An airgun lay on a shelf. It was inconceivable that anybody could miss. The booth was unattended.

'Oh, please let me have a try at the swans. It's only fifty pence.'

'Well, only one. Understand?'

Her childishness was so ludicrous it was almost funny. He wondered if she were trying to entertain him.

The pasty old woman smiled conspiratorially as she took his money.

'Wouldn't the kind gentleman care to have a go?'

Esther held the rod she had been given with awe, as if at any minute she expected it to turn into a snake.

'What do I do now?'

'Just catch hold of one of the little swans, dearie.'

The swans bobbed about on the water impervious to

154

Esther's proddings, propelled partly by her inexpertise and partly by the buffeting wind.

'Come on, Esther, this is ridiculous, all you've got to do is hook the bloody thing.'

He was annoyed; annoyed that he had been bamboozled into letting her play the fatuous game, annoyed that she was being so ineffectual and annoyed because he was cold to the bone.

'That's all right, don't let your father put you off. Take your time.'

Esther giggled nervously. Arthur wanted to correct the old woman but couldn't think how to without sounding absurdly prissy.

'Nearly, ever so nearly. Quite an art to it, isn't there?'

A small cluster of children had gathered round and watched Esther's bungling with scorn. She turned to Arthur, completely unaware of the fool she was making of herself, and gave him a radiant smile.

'That's it, dearie, gently now. Oh, well done!'

The old woman took the rod from Esther and unhooked the recalcitrant plastic swan. She turned it over and examined its base.

'No prize, after all that! Oh, I am truly sorry, love.'

'Right, come on, Esther, let's go, we've wasted enough time.'

Esther didn't move. Arthur pulled her arm roughly, but she stood her ground.

'Please, Arthur, just one more turn. I know how to do it now.'

To his astonishment he saw that she was on the verge of tears.

'What's wrong with you? Are you crazy?'

'Please, I beg you.'

Angrily Arthur flung the money on to the board. The children, bewildered, withdrew.

'Better luck this time, dearie.'

Arthur turned away. He was quivering with rage. Such spoilt behaviour in anyone over the age of three was incredible, in someone of her age it was unforgivable. He was seized by an urge to punish her. He wanted to hit her, slap her freckled, puppy-fat cheeks, whip her till she wept. He hid his shaking hands in his pockets. He couldn't bear to look at her.

155

'That's it, softly softly, catchee monkey.'

'It's not a monkey,' he murmured to himself, 'it's a swan, you stupid old fool.'

He looked back and saw that he had wandered. His heart was still pounding. He breathed in and out deeply. His fury was beginning to ease. Sadly he realized that he had been acting as childishly as she, but he couldn't understand why she had made him so violently angry.

'Go on, dearie, that's the way. Oh, aren't you the clever one.'

For no apparent reason he suddenly thought of Bel. He saw her propped up in her hospital bed with Briar standing beside her. It was really their faces he saw, hers battered, his harrowed. Something that Briar had once asked him came to mind. 'You know those paintings of Bel's, reckon they're worth anything?' His reflections puzzled him, he could perceive no pretext for them, nor any real connection. It was certainly surprising that Briar had taken the uncharacteristic step of visiting his great aunt in hospital. But what did that prove? Then with horror he glimpsed the emergence of a most monstrous notion.

'Oh, I am glad, love, you've won a prize. Didn't I say, "Patience has its own reward"? Now what colour do you fancy?'

Esther ran up to him, all trace of her obduracy effaced. She was still a child, but an excited and happy one.

'Arthur, look!'

She held a mauve doll up to him. She was as proud as a mother showing off her first-born. He stared at it, wondering whether she expected him to kiss it.

'Are you still cross with me?'

'No, I'm OK now.'

'Are you sure? Don't look worried.'

'It's nothing. It's banished.'

She stood on tiptoe and brushed her lips against his cheek.

'It's just that it's the first fun-fair I've ever been to and I did so want to win a prize to give to my mother.'

'It wasn't much of a fair, you know.'

'I don't care. I loved it.'

Esther tripped on ahead of him, 'gay and innocent and

156

heartless'. He felt he was about to be overwhelmed by the burgeoning suspicion he had conceived but couldn't suppress. Could Briar, his own son, really have been capable of such barbarity?

'Arthur, that must be the fort the policeman was talking about.'

Brick walled and topped with stone it lay low on the flat land. The stuff of history. Esther was already peopling it in her mind with knights in armour and clattering horses and eager young squires.

'Why don't we go and explore?'

'Do you really want to? I've rather had this place.'

'But you haven't found what you were looking for yet.'

'Oh I have, sort of.'

'What is it?'

With a flourish of his hand he encompassed Tilbury, the river, the marshes, the factories, Esther's doll.

'All this nothingness.'

'My father says ... '

She stopped. She suspected he no longer cared what her father said.

They passed a gatehouse with an ornate Carolean stone façade, beyond was a tall door that swung to and fro in the wind.

'Shall we go in? It's deserted.'

In front of them was an immense sunken courtyard surrounded by grass mounds. At the far end stood a terrace of trim houses. Massive, obsolete cannons ringed the area, facing inwards.

Esther caught sight of a flight of wooden steps.

'Do you think we're allowed up?'

At the top was a parapet overlooking the river and a small red-bricked building designated 'Chapel'.

'God, it's cold! Aren't you frozen, Esther?'

'History's always fascinated me.'

They tried the door of the chapel but it was locked. Arthur rattled the handle.

'Typical!'

'You two haven't got tickets. It's fifty pence each.'

A small man, aggrandized by his heavy, dark blue overcoat, had stolen up on them.

157

'Came in the back, I suppose. That's devious.'

He wore a peaked cap with a badge on it and jangled a large ring of keys as he spoke.

'No deception intended, I assure you. Here's a pound.'

'You'll want to see the chapel, that's why it's kept shut up. Don't worry, it's no skin off my back.'

Loose-fitting teeth gave the man an inane and permanent grin that failed to belie his surliness. He unlocked the door. Inside, puritan austerity reigned: highly polished pews, a severely simple altar table and two candlesticks.

'There's not much to see. It's them ruddy children, proper little vandals. Had enough?'

Outside he pointed to a church tower on the horizon.

'Near there Queen Elizabeth addressed her troops before the Armada in 1588 or 1598. I'm no good at dates. I'm not local, I'm from up north.'

'What else is there to see?'

'There's the museum. Mind you, there's not a lot in it, but you can read the names of the Jacobite prisoners they had here. Over three hundred of them. Then there's the powder magazines. Some folk think they're interesting, but they're mostly locked up. Pardon me.'

He put an index finger in his mouth and rootled about between gum and denture. His search over, he resumed grinning and aimed the same finger at a spot to the left of the row of houses.

'If you want to take a look inside there's one open over there. Just look for a red door. Funny thing about Queen Elizabeth, it wasn't this one, you know, it was the other one.'

Arthur and Esther stood at the bottom of the steps.

'Had enough?'

'We might as well get our money's-worth.'

They crossed the courtyard. Ahead of them was a thin gully cut into the embankment and at the end an open, red door.

'What's the betting it reeks of cats?'

'It looks spooky, do we have to go in?'

'Esther, it was your idea, not mine.'

Beyond the threshold was a very long brick-lined passage feebly lit.

'Shall we go in?'

158

'I don't know. I'll stick with you.'

The air inside was unexpectedly dry and fresh. As they proceeded down the narrow passage they saw why: primitive ventilation shafts pierced the ceiling. At regular intervals there were empty, whitewashed rooms.

'You were wrong, it doesn't smell of cats at all.'

'It's staggering! Esther, this passage must be fifty yards long. It reminds me of nightmares I used to have about infinity.'

'I hate the thought of infinity.'

'That can't be very orthodox of you.'

The passage turned a corner and went on, seemingly for ever. The sound of their steps on the stone-flagged floor was menacingly deadened.

'Esther, this is it! This is what I was looking for. Hell will be like this, perhaps this is hell.'

He laughed and turned to her to join in his merriment. But she was not there. One minute she had been with him, now she was gone. He stood still. There was no sound. He shouted her name. His voice was swallowed up. He ran back down the passage looking into all the empty, whitewashed rooms. At any moment he expected to find her, hiding behind a wall or in a recess, laughing at his concern and her own childish trickery. But she was nowhere. He reached the entrance and leant against the door breathless. A regular drip of water oozed from the brickwork above him and splashed at his feet. He wondered if he were already dead.

Out of the burrow, with the open sky and courtyard before him, he felt saner. There was no sign of Esther: the only figure in sight was that of the blue-coated custodian. Feigning calm Arthur approached him.

'You haven't by any chance seen my friend?'

'Friend?'

'Yes, I've lost her.'

'I'm sorry to hear it.'

'Have you seen her? She was with me in the powder magazine just a few minutes ago.'

'What's she look like?'

'She's in white, short with mousy hair.'

'Continental type?'

'Sort of.'

'No, I can't help you. My trouble is I'm no good at faces. See that church tower over there. In 1588 or 1598 Queen Elizabeth addressed her troops before the Armada from thereabouts. Funny isn't it?'

'But you must remember. You sold us both tickets and then showed us round the chapel. It was less than an hour ago. She was dressed in white.'

'I'm always opening up the chapel, it's part of my job. People are just people to me, I don't look at their faces. I'm not local, I'm from up north.'

Arthur pushed him aside. He ran on, past the tall swinging door that they had entered by, past the Carolean gatehouse and on towards the river. Rounding a quoin of the fort he saw her at once, white against the grey sky. She was up on the embankment, a gangly butterfly, staring across at the water. He was about to shout to her when he felt the return of an old friend, the cauterizing pain in his back, the truest companion he had ever known. She looked down and waved to him to come up and then she ran along the footpath away from him. He stopped. The anguish was still there. He spoke softly, to the sky, to the river, to Tilbury: 'This time it will not pass me by, not this time.' Esther was fading away. Now so far away she was little more than a cipher.